D0825147

Society Vs You

Play The Game Your Way!

Sunni T. Connor

Naturally Sunni

Edited by William Hunt

Facebook: www.facebook.com/sunnitconnor

Instagram: www.instagram.com/sunni_theauthor/

Website: www.sunnitconnor.com

DEDICATION

I dedicate this book to my beautiful children. To my daughter, Terrah: You are gorgeous in your skin, your spirit is kind, and your heart is pure. To my son Zi'yas: You are confident, respectful, and fearless. The two of you have given me one amazing gift. Now let's play this game to win!

To Mr. Carver: To infinity and beyond, while we are in these bodies. To my parents: I thank you for creating me and supporting my journey every step of the way.

Contents

INTRODUCTION

Here's the truth. I had this long introduction written out for you, and it was amazing! At the last minute, though, I deleted it, because what you are about to read is so outside of the box, not even I could explain it in a four-page introduction.

But what I *can* tell you is that the message of this book has played a huge part of my existence on this planet. I'm here to relay this message to as many people who are willing to hear it.

So, what is the message? Simply put, the message is that there is a version of yourself that your ego created based on society's expectations, and there is also a version of yourself that you *really* are. Both of these versions create conflict because your true self will never accept the version of you that others expect to see.

Your true self will continue to pull you toward your own destiny, but if you resist, you will feel like you are not enough. The truth is, though, you were born more than enough. You are likely competing with a false identity built by society, and I'm here to bring you back to your true self.

My methods are not conventional, but I promise you will get what you need from this book. My higher self, the *real me,* can tap into something far beyond this reality, but my ego-self, my *false identity,* held on to the life lessons I've learned when I lived in Society's world. Together they created magic, and that's what you are holding in your hands: pure magic.

1

We Are Vibration

"We are vibrational beings; we're not just flesh and blood. You cannot have what you're not willing to become vibrationally."

~Michael Beckwith

Where do we come from?

WE COME FROM A SOURCE OF POWERFUL ENERGY. It's bigger than what the eye can see, yet this source is our vision, our heartbeat, our everything. I know some of us really thought we came from our father's testicles during a sexual encounter with our mother. That's partially true, but more importantly, we come from a speck of invisible power.

This invisible power exists naturally in every one of us! It's making your heart beat right now and enabling your eyes to read these words, and it will soon tell your hand to flip the page. At this very moment, are you telling yourself to breathe? This invisible power is helping you breathe even when you are not thinking about it.

You are that special! There will never be another you! It would be a waste of universal intelligence to take the time to create a duplicate *you*. Nope, you're it! You don't get another chance to be made over. You have to become the version of yourself you want to be, with the energy that resides in you right now.

What Society Tells Us

WE WERE TOLD WE MUST DO THIS AND DO THAT, work here and work there. No one told us the truth. Many don't know the truth. Life has been a pattern of old remedies and lessons learned from our ancestors. You know them all so well, like religion. Our religion was pretty much chosen for us at birth. Generation after generation. I was a Christian before I could even say, "ma ma." Why? Who said I wanted to be a Christian? Who said my inner self wanted to be religious at all?

Society chose for us, because according to society, we must fit into a group. Society put me in the black group, the poor group, the Christian group, the urban group, the hood group, or whatever other group they relate to African Americans. By the way, it's always been hard for me to accept the title "African American" as a race. It's more like a reminder. A reminder of the Africans that were enslaved in America. It's that kind of title that encourages separation from the human race. We are human beings that have the same organs as any other human being on this planet. We don't have to accept society's unjustified labels. But we do. We often comply. Instead of accepting the titles placed on us, let's recognize who and what we really are.

The Truth!

SO WHAT'S THE TRUTH? We are born into this vibrational universe with the purpose of experiencing life in a short period of time. We came here with power within. Everything you need is inside you right now. Nothing outside us can fulfill our needs; we must look inward first.

Don't believe me? Think about a glass of water. Picture getting the glass out of your kitchen cabinet. Imagine the ice cubes filling the top of the glass while you run the faucet to allow the water to get cold. You could get up right now and pour yourself a glass of water if you chose.

That is the power within us. We have the power of imagination. We can think about it, desire it, imagine it, and then go get it.

Screw what society says your limits are. If you can see it, you can have it. Funny enough, if you can't see it, you still can have it. If you want the water and you can imagine the water, your mind will guide you to get the water. Then you can drink it, no matter what stereotype or race you are.

That was a very simple example of how easy life can be when you change your mindset. Was it hard to picture a glass of water? I'm sure it wasn't. Would it be hard to get the water? I'm sure it wouldn't be. So why do we make life so hard? Why do we allow others to determine our fate? Why do we still fall in line and do what we think we must do?

It's time to open your mind. I will need you to be completely open while reading the rest of this book. Remember, this book is a free space, with no religion, rules, cults, family beliefs, or bullshit fed to us by society. Just you and I. Let's open our minds to imagine what LIFE could be, which is what I believe life is supposed to be.

The Proposed Game

YOU ARE A SPIRIT IN A BODY. Correct? Let's say a higher spirit proposed a game you could play that would allow you to experience life. The deal was simple: You get to come to earth to experience life. But there were a few stipulations before you agreed. Your spirit had to agree to come to Earth in bodily form (a baby) with no knowledge.

This baby would have to learn to play the game on their own with no memory of the returned place. The baby would have to learn to walk, talk, read, feel, and experience. Babies are the most aligned humans on the planet. Babies don't get discouraged when their first attempts to crawl or walk don't work. They don't get embarrassed and tell themselves they'll never succeed. They just keep trying, no matter what, like it's impossible for them NOT to succeed.

You too are like the babies, you just forgot. While playing this game, you'd get to create, have fun, feel emotions, taste different foods, learn to love, and interact with other humans, but most importantly you'd get to live the experience.

Now before this higher power threw you into the game, it gave you one very special power to go along with you. That power is your spirit, also known as your inner being. Your spirit started this game with you, and no matter what illusions or challenges life (the game) may show you, you will always have your power within you. You came to the game with your spirit to experience life. Another stipulation is you will have to die and ultimately leave the game. You will return back to your beginning place with your spirit. Everyone in the game dies.

Here's how the game works. You get no clues when you first enter this world. You came in eager, emotionless, and without much knowledge. Sadly, people throw their beliefs on you at a young age before you start playing the game your own way. The game of life works like this: You can do whatever you want to do. You are here for a short period of time to do whatever you want to do. It's that simple.

You can create a new invention if you choose. You can create change in the world if you choose. You can reproduce more humans if you choose. You can choose to serve. You can have an erotic experience. You can be a 9-5 slave. You can play the game however you want, but there are rules to any game.

The rules in life are simple. You get to have an experience, and then you die. These are facts and these are the basic rules. There are the laws of the universe, which we'll discuss later in this chapter, but they are laws, not rules. How you play this game of endless possibilities is totally up to you. To allow anyone to control your game (life) is a total waste of an experience.

The Voice

NEVER QUIT THE GAME, NEVER GIVE UP (commit suicide or fall into depression) or you automatically surrender your power to the game. The easiest way to beat the game is to remember that you are a spirit first. Stop listening to others who don't know anything about what you feel inside. Listen to that voice inside you. It's the really strong voice, not all those other crazy voices that you picked up from society. You know the voice. The voice that told you not to touch the fire on the stove when you were only two years old. The voice that told you not to go to college to be a nurse just because your family said so. The voice that told you to pick up this book. That voice is always there and it's always stronger than the random voices that appear in your thoughts.

It's very important to find and listen to your inner being (the voice). Your inner being is your navigation through the game. Your inner being is attached to all that is. It's God, it's the universe, it's the trees, it's the dirt on the earth, it's the heartbeat of a lion, it's connected to all. Why? Because in this vibrational reality called life, we all agreed to play the game, so we are all connected to the experience.

Before we move forward, I must address something that was hard for me to grasp conceptually. That is, we are vibrational beings living in a vibrational universe. That is a truth I still have to remind myself of daily. We produce signals that attract our vibration, which in turn manifests whatever we want in the game. This is so important, but sadly it's easily forgotten.

Why is vibration so important? If we can understand vibration, then we can begin to understand how life works and we can ultimately play the game to win. Some people are just on the board, but they are not playing, so they can never win. If you can think of a desire, then you can send out a vibrational signal that matches it, and then it can manifest. If you don't turn your own thoughts into things, then society will do it for you. Consequently, you will find yourself living off other people's vibrations, and you will ultimately be unhappy.

STORYTIME

"Who am I?"

I am a speck of energy. I spent a lot of time alone as a child. That time I spent alone resulted in me really getting to know myself. I grew up in the projects, also known as public housing. The projects were always noisy and filled with chaos, but I learned how to find stillness in my room. I first started reading obsessively and that blocked out the noise, but when the book was over, the noise always returned.

Whenever I was outside playing, I loved the hood chatter. It wasn't until I was alone that I yearned for silence. I was about six years old when I realized I was more than just a body; I was more than flesh. I was the annoying kid that asked a million questions and the adults often complained about me "talking too much!" My mother is a beautiful person that I simply adore, but mothers get annoyed too.

I'll never forget the day I met myself for the very first time. I ran into my mother's room, where she sat on the end of the bed enjoying her Newport 100, flipping through the stations of her old box television.

"Hey, Mommy. Can I ask you a question?"

"Sure baby, what's up?"

"Who am I?"

My mother glanced at me with confusion. "Girl, what do you mean?" she asked, her eyes skipping back to the television.

"I mean like, what am I?" I asked, flopping onto her bed.

"You are a person, Sunni," she answered, now looking at me instead of the television.

"What's a person?" I asked with big curious eyes.

"A human. You have flesh, skin, and bones. You are a person. What are you talking about?" Quickly, she smashed her cigarette butt into the ashtray, realizing I had more to ask.

"I mean, what else are we? Like, who is talking to you right now? It can't be my lips. It has to be something making my lips move," I adamantly protested.

"It's your brain, baby. Your mind is making your lips move. We are humans, Sunni. Is that all?" she asked with a slight annoyance.

"No. Who's controlling my brain?"

She raised her eyebrows. "I don't know, Sunni. How about you go back into your room and play. You know I don't like you around smoke."

"But you are not smoking anymore," I protested.

My mother gave me the "*Don't play with me, girl*" look, so I left her room and shut the door. I quietly mumbled to myself, "Adults never know the answers."

I went into my room and found silence. For some reason or another, no one was outside yelling at that precise moment. I looked at my hands and asked out loud, "Who are you?" I remember feeling something magical. I thought I was special for feeling the bliss of the room. I later realized we all have this special power inside us. Everything was perfect. I met my soul that day. Not my brain, which is like a machine. The brain remembers things, like this memory I just shared with you. Not my mind, which thinks random thoughts, but can also build ships if I want it to.

It was my special power, my soul, my spirit, my inner being, it was the God in me. It was the voice. That's who we are.

To this day, if I forget who I am, I can look at my hands and bring myself right back to that day when I met my soul. It's something greater inside of us, and that power can tap into the universe's power. Our souls never left the magical place we originated from. It's there and *here*. It's trying to get you to your goals, but if you never listen, how will you hear it? The path is already there for you, and the soul knows the way. Listen to your inner being, not the world, and you will reach every desire you can imagine.

The Law Of Attraction

I OFTEN TRY TO TALK ABOUT THE LAW OF ATTRACTION TO PEOPLE. They either have no knowledge of what I'm talking about or disregard what I'm saying because it feels too weird. Please don't do that here. It's important to know that there are laws in the universe. I need you to keep that fresh in your mind as you are living this experience.

We like to follow the common laws of the universe, such as the law of gravity. You wouldn't get on an elevator and go to the roof of a building and jump with the intention to fly. Gravity will slap you straight to the ground. You follow these laws of the universe because they seem more logical for some reason. But we tend to ignore some of the most important laws of the game.

The Law of Attraction is one of, if not the most, important laws in the universe. So what is this Law of Attraction? Simply put, what you focus on with thought, emotion, and intention is what you get. The universe brings you like-minded things.

Imagine your thoughts are like magnets. One magnet will gravitate toward another magnet (a like-minded thought). You think of a new house and you feel the emotion of how nice it would be to have a new house for your family. The Law of Attraction will send you like-minded thoughts. It will move the players on the board to the right place at the right time for your desires.

The tricky part is that there are no exclusions. Meaning, if your thought is contradictory, the Law of Attraction will take the thought that has the most emotion, and that's what you'll get. For example, if you say, "I want a new house, BUT I'm scared of having a mortgage." Which emotion is stronger? The excitement of a new house or the fear of the mortgage? If it's the fear of the mortgage, the Law of Attraction will give you more fear because that's your vibration. If it's the excitement of the new house and you keep that excitement, baby, you will get a new house. It is LAW!

How Do Thoughts Become Things?

THOUGHTS ARE VIBRATIONS. When you think a thought, it sends a signal and the universe immediately finds a matching signal. So let's play this out because I really want you to understand this.

There is a man named Michael who works at a bank, and he has not been meeting his deadlines at work. In the last few months, he has only signed up one customer for a home loan. Instead of being down on himself, he thinks of signing up many customers so he won't lose his job.

15

I want to get better at work, he thinks. I know I can do more loans. I love my job. I want that Christmas bonus. It's plenty of people that need a house. I'll do more research. Yup, I got this.

So we clearly see Michael's vibration. He wants to keep the job he loves and he wants to put more people in houses. Now, fifteen miles away, there's a lady named Lisa who is renting from a slum landlord, but all she has ever wanted was to be a homeowner.

I want a new house so bad, she thinks. I can't wait to grow flowers on my front lawn. I think I want to make one of the bedrooms into an office. I just got that raise, so maybe now I can afford it. I'm off work today. My friend said it's a buyer's market. I'll go to the bank today, then I'll look for a real estate agent. Yup, I got this.

Now, we clearly see Lisa's vibration. She wants to manifest a house. She was previously afraid of owning a home, but now she is talking to herself with confidence. This is when the Law of Attraction works the best! Neither person has doubt, just clear, precise thoughts on what they want, and the universe is eager to give it to them.

One day, everyone on Michael's team decides to go out for lunch, but he is so focused on keeping his job that he decides to stay behind and research. Lisa walks in the door without an appointment, requesting to speak with someone about a loan for a house. Michael greets her and brings her into his office. They run into a few problems with her credit, but he's so dedicated to keeping his job that he thinks outside the box and gets her approved.

The Law of Attraction took the vibration of Michael's thoughts and matched it to the vibration of Lisa's thoughts. Because there was no doubt from either party, the manifestation happened quickly. Michael would've missed Lisa had he gone out to lunch with his co-workers instead of following his intuition, and Lisa probably wouldn't have gotten approved that day, had she not worked with Michael, who was so dedicated.

A lot of times we ask for things, but then shut them down with doubt in the same sentence. There is no favoritism in the universe; it follows the laws. People who appear to be doing much better than others in life simply **think** better. They have more confidence in what they want, and they hold their desires with strong attention, making it easy for the universe to provide them with a manifestation.

The Word "BUT"

Can we cancel the word **but**? There is no BUT! Everything you want in your life that you are not getting is because of the word BUT. I can promise you that the words that come after the word BUT are why you are not living up to your fullest potential.

Examples:

- I want to move to Texas **but** I don't know anyone there.

- I want to start my own clothing line **but** there are too many competitors.

- I want to ask for a raise **but** the company just gave raises last quarter.

I can go on and on, but you get the point. Did you notice I used *but* in the previous sentence? If you did, I see you are paying attention. Just had to throw that out there. Let's drop every word after the word **but** from the previous examples.

New Examples:

- I want to move to Texas.

- I want to start my own clothing line.

- I want to ask for a raise.

See the difference? Because there's no contradiction or doubt, the universe can provide you with more like-minded thoughts based on your vibration. So let me show how your next thoughts can go by removing BUT and replacing it with positive thoughts. Or another option is to purposely think with confidence.

Positive Examples:

- I want to move to Texas. I heard the rent was cheap. It's an entirely new world out there, and it's time I explore it. It will be so fun to meet new people.

- I want to start my own clothing line. Nobody makes clothes like me. It will be so dope to see people in my attire.

- I want to ask for a raise. I work hard. I deserve more compensation. I'm sure there's more money in the budget. I'll show my supervisor all the money I made the company last quarter, and they'll surely consider giving me a raise.

Wow, what a difference. These are easy commands, and keeping them active in your mind will make them happen quicker. Please keep in mind that things take time, and you want them to. Trust me. If you received everything you thought about right away, this world would be even more insane. Imagine wanting a baby, and two seconds after having the thought you were holding a crying baby in your arms. That's too fast. Let life take you on your journey. It's what makes it worth living.

The easiest way to remember to be patient with the things you want is to think about planting corn. First, you have to plant the seed (have the thought), then water the soil (do the action), let it grow (wait on the universe), and take a bite of the sweet corn (enjoy the manifestation).

I never intended to get this deep on this topic, but these are things many of us don't know. These are the things we need to know in order to question society's rules. The Law of Attraction changed my life. I get anything and everything I want. I have to share this, so you can too. We have to change our limiting beliefs. It's just the same story you've been telling yourself, but believe me, there's much more out there. Open your mind as you read this book, and I promise you will never be the same.

In summary, where we come from doesn't matter as much as what we came with. We came with infinite power, and it works endlessly. We came with the power to vibrate to whatever we want. We came here to create, to be great, to invent, to achieve, to learn, and most importantly to experience.

There are two times when being a follower is acceptable. *You can follow to lead, and you can follow to learn.* All other times you must only follow your own inner being. Who cares about what the other humans are doing? We came here to leave our own mark on this universe. Choosing society's version of yourself will only leave you with a life that is a shell of what you hoped it would be.

2

Fear Is An Illusion

"The brave man is not he who does not feel afraid, but he who conquers that fear."

~ Nelson Mandela

Facing Fear

FEAR IS WHAT HOLDS MOST OF US BACK FROM OUR TRUE DESIRES. Think about the first time you drove a car. You sat in the driver's seat, your heart pounding uncontrollably. You pulled the seat belt over your shoulder, and when you heard the click you knew it was secure. You nervously fixed all the mirrors, taking extra time to procrastinate because you were scared to death to start the ignition. You asked whoever was assisting you a bunch of dumb questions just to waste a little more time before you put your foot on the brake pedal.

Eventually you turned the car on, put the car in drive even though your heart was pumping with anxiety, then slowly released the brake, your adrenaline slowing down as you realized the car was moving. You felt immediate relief, and with a big smile you thought, "I'm driving." A few weeks later, you got into your car with no fear and just drove. You made fear your servant, which is the only way to achieve your goals in life.

Once you conquer fear, it will go away until the next challenging goal. Now that you know how to drive, are you afraid? No! You just do it. Here's a secret about fear: It's actually a good thing. It's the way your mind has been programmed to push you to do uncomfortable things to get you to a higher level.

Real Fear

THE ONLY *REAL* FEAR YOU SHOULD EVER BE AFRAID OF IS REAL DANGER. If you are swimming in the middle of the ocean on a nice vacation and a gray fin starts circling you, you should be afraid. If you happen to find yourself standing in front of a wild lion, you should be frightened. If the pilot of a plane says, "Sorry, passengers, but we are making an emergency landing because the plane has run out of gas," you should be scared. These are examples of when your fight or flight mode should kick in. These are scary situations in which your human form should feel fear in order to protect you.

Fake Fear

HOW DOES SOCIETY SCARE YOU, ON THE OTHER HAND? Oh, they say you can't do this, you can't do that. Don't quit that job because you have three kids to support. Keep your head out of the clouds and get a real job. Don't leave your husband; he is the breadwinner, and things will get better. Get married before you have kids. Go to church every Sunday. Don't move out of the state for that job—you don't know anyone there. Don't start a business—most fail within the first five years.

These are fake fears because you are not in any real danger. You are playing the game of life as a weak player. You are letting society tell you to be afraid of the things you should be doing. You should be living. You should take pleasure in taking risks, because you won't be here forever and the worst thing that could happen is you create a new experience.

Society tells you these things because the average person is scared to death of risk. Most people are terrified of change or any type of challenge involving growth. Why? They are scared humans that have been following the other humans' rules for too long. They prefer to stay comfortable. Comfortability is safe, but unfortunately, staying comfortable won't get you far in the game. You make the same money your entire life and do the same boring things. No judgment from me if that's what you want, but it's surely not what your soul desires.

If you are comfortable dying comfortably, then that's your choice. If, though, you want to actually leave your mark, saying "I WAS HERE!" then don't let society's fear hold you back. Many people are scared to dream or to change. NOT YOU! The fact that you are holding in your hands a book called "Society vs You" tells me that you have courage. You are ready to leave the bubble of mediocrity. I know you wake up knowing there is more to life. There is! I promise it's whatever you want it to be.

Be An Animal, Or Not!

WE SHARE THIS UNIVERSE WITH MANY DIFFERENT CREATURES AND CREATIONS. Imagine you are looking at the game board of life from above in the sky. You would see a lot of trees waving, cars moving, planes flying, people that look as small as ants, birds soaring, and lights twinkling. You would be looking at the sum total of all of our thoughts manifested into this reality called life. Someone invented cars, planes, lights, buildings, and so on. Nature was created by the master of the game, it was built into the game board, and it will be here even when we are not. The tree next to your house will possibly outlive you, but you don't even say hello to the tree. You walk past it like it's nothing, but nature is built into the game, which is why if you can find yourself lost in nature, you usually can come back to your true self.

The animals are living the experience of life as well. Some even refer to humans as animals. I admire the animals because they don't stress or worry. They just "be." They just are who they are. They are fully connected to the universe. They know the universe provides abundance. A lion never worries if it will eat. It just searches until it finds food. The lion doesn't stress to the point that he can't roar, or lose sleep from lack of faith. He knows he will eat again because the infinite power that controls all things will answer his desires in massive amounts. There will surely be another gazelle. That is what we must learn from the animals. We must learn to just be, to flow with the knowing that everything is here for us.

Why all this talk about animals? I'm speaking about animals for two reasons.

1. We can learn to just "BE" from them.

2. We can recognize we have something the animals don't have, and that's the power of the mind.

Being a person in this vibrational universe and living like an animal can be beneficial in the sense of relaxing and flowing with the flow of life. HOWEVER, we should never get into a static routine the way the animals do. We came here with a powerful tool called the brain, which works with the heart and the spirit. We must use it, just like you're using it right now to read these words.

Reading these words, though, is not using your brain to its fullest potential. Your brain has previously memorized letters, words, and sounds, so reading these words is like a program in your brain. You are not thinking, you are following a learned pattern that does not require new thoughts. I want you to *think*! I want you to create new thoughts. I want you to imagine the life you want, detail for detail, and create it with your mind, then apply action.

Animals are smart, but we were designed to be *brilliant*! The game of life actually doesn't care how smart you are. You are not special because of your IQ; you are special because you are "you." Geniuses waste their knowledge every day living regular mediocre lives. I know really smart people who work dead-end jobs. We have the power in our minds to manifest any desire we could ever imagine, and we can learn any skill we can imagine.

My question to you is this: Are you going to be an animal and live life in a routine? Or are you going to be an infinite being with the power to do the impossible and "BE" as the animals are? Will you be afraid to take risks? Will you wake up and robotically do the exact same things? Do you feel like fear is holding you back? Are you afraid to take a chance and actually live? What did you come here for? If you forgot, let me remind you. You came here to be great, and as long as you remember fear is your BITCH, nothing and no one can stop you.

———*ell*———

STORYTIME

"Scared"

I had the brilliant idea to be a motivational speaker because I found myself having an impact on people when I opened my mouth. People really listened to me, and it was rewarding to watch people make jumps in life and take risks.

One day, after I had finished meditating, I came up with the idea to send my first book, *DAMAGED little girl*, to all the prisons in the U.S. That was a huge goal and I didn't even know where to start. I started calling prisons and being transferred and told "NO" a lot. After much persistence, many of the prisons started allowing my books into their library, and I built relationships in the process. The women inmates at the Jessup Correctional Facility loved my book so much that the librarian and the warden asked if I could come in person to speak to the women. I created a program for the prison talk called, "Forget your old story!"

I arrived at the prison and was told to remove all of my jewelry and take off my shoes and do this and that. I was nervous. It wasn't my first time visiting a prison to see an inmate, but this time I was there to motivate. I started doubting myself. What did I have to offer women who'd had their freedom stripped away from them? What motivation could I possibly give them while they were incarcerated? I knew I'd had a rough life, but I had no experience of what it felt like to be in that situation. I was already there and had committed to the talk, though, and I wasn't going to back out.

I walked into the room and spoke to the librarian. The warden greeted me and asked me not to use profanity, and told me that everything else was in my control. The women inmates were loud, rowdy, and talkative as they came in. Some of them peeked at me, and some of them just took their seats. A few were setting up the room, and they came over and told me how much they loved my book and how relatable it was. That eased my nerves just a little bit.

It was time for me to go on stage. I heard so much noise, it reminded me of the project chatter when I was younger. I knew the only way I could get the women to listen to me was to get the room back. I was scared shitless. My underarms were sweating, my right hand was shaking, and I had forgotten most of what I planned to talk about. For about twenty seconds I was under fear's control, and then I stepped on the stage. Most of them ignored me and kept talking.

With the mic in my hand, I said, "Thank y'all for coming to hear me speak. Now I need y'all to shut up so you can get this knowledge." I smiled. They smiled back and gave me their undivided attention. The room became silent.

My hand stopped shaking and I felt my body calm down. The butterflies were less intense. I had the room back, and suddenly all their eyes were on me and I talked my stuff. I broke all the rules, I used profanity, and I got gutter with them so they could feel my energy. In the end, not only did I get a standing ovation but the entire staff that was in the room worshiped my talk as well. They weren't even upset that I had cursed, and I smiled to myself and said, "Yeah, Fear, you're still my Bitch."

As of today, I've done more than twenty public speaking events since then and I still get nervous, but I no longer am afraid to speak publicly. The fear died that day.

Fear Creates Power

WHEN I WAS A LITTLE GIRL, I CONSTANTLY FELT FEAR. I wasn't a scaredy-cat or afraid of the dark. I was afraid of life and the unknown. My heart would beat fast if someone called my name aggressively, if someone wanted to fight, or even if someone loudly knocked on our front door. My fear was not based on real danger, but on the illusion of something being wrong. I created this illusion in my mind. To be honest, that little girl still exists in me. I have to remind her everything is okay and there's nothing to fear.

We've been talking about life as if it's a board game, and as you know, in many board games there's always a little fear. In Monopoly you are afraid to land on someone's property. In Sorry you are afraid someone will knock you off your spot. In Trouble you are afraid you won't get a six or a one to get out.

Why do you think those games were designed with the intent to scare you or prepare you for something to go wrong? Because it's fun. It's fun to not know what's going to happen, and it's also scary. Imagine the feeling you get when you are playing Monopoly and you only have three hundred dollars and you skip over Boardwalk, which is loaded with properties. You get extremely excited, right? The other player didn't get you that time. First you felt fear, then excitement. That's why fear is power.

Behind every fast heartbeat is the power to evolve. Every time something scares you and you do that thing anyway, you become a higher version of yourself and you gain power because that thing you feared is no longer scary. It can't control you because now you know what it is. The unknown is what scares us the most, and if we don't face it, we often get left behind.

Every successful person takes many risks. They face fears repeatedly. They don't know if they are making a bad investment, which is scary, but they make the investment anyway, and after they do that once or twice the fear is gone, even if they lose the money.

I wish I had a shortcut answer to avoiding fear, but there isn't one. You have to use the key to open the door. Keys are specially made. Your parents can't do it for you, your coaches can't do it for you; only you can face your fears, only you have the key. On the other side of the door is power. It's impossible to accomplish your dreams without facing a lot of fear.

Some of the opposites of fear are courage and self-confidence. Actually, I speak more about self-confidence in Chapter 7, so let's just focus on courage. The definition of courage is the ability to do something that frightens you. It takes courage to live this life *YOUR* way. An easy way to gain courage is to remind yourself that if you do the thing that scares you, the worst that can happen is NOT death, so you'll still be here to try again. You get another turn to roll the dice. There is no wrong way to do life; you always get another chance to try again. Don't let fear cripple you. Roll the dice and step into the unknown, where all your power awaits you.

3

Forget Your Old Story

"I don't have a story. Everybody wants this Holly-wood story, but the world don't owe you nothing, man. It's what you owe the world."

~ Bernie Mac

Forget Your Old Story

STORIES MATTER, RIGHT? Every time you meet someone new, you probably tell them some old story about yourself. Where you used to live, how you used to dress, how your previous relationship ended, how your mother treated you as a child, and what career you left behind.

To hell with your old story! Stop telling it! Stop being the victim and stop living in those horrific moments. Even if your old story is a good story, still stop telling it. We only have this moment, right here and right now. There is so much harm in telling an old story over and over again. One thing that happens is your brain keeps reliving that same story. It has a permanent place in your mind, and you never know when a trigger may happen. It's holding you back from true happiness.

Your story is an illusion because you're not capable of remembering those stories one hundred percent accurately. Emotion is added to the story, and you start having a selective memory about what actually happened. It's also an illusion because if it's not in this moment, that time has passed. In order to tell an old story, you must rely on memory because it's not actually happening right now, which means it doesn't actually exist. It only exists in your mind, because that time in space is gone.

This quote says it best:

"You cannot suffer the past or the future because they do not exist. What you are suffering is your memory and your imagination." Sadhguru

Everything you've been through has made you who you are. Only use those memories to remind yourself of who you really are. You don't have to *be* that story. I don't care if you used to be the biggest drug dealer in the city, a murderer, a prostitute, a wife, a corporate genius, a bad parent, or anything else; you don't have to be that story anymore. Whether it was a good or bad story, remember you are constantly evolving! Life is about growth, and you are in a new time-space reality that has a new story for you. It will be hard for you to match the vibration of the new story if you are stuck in the past.

Weirdly enough, I'm about to tell an old story. What a hypocrite I am! This quick story will explain how telling an old story almost made me miss out on a lot of French toast.

STORYTIME

"Why I hated eggs"

When I was about four years old, there was a girl named Keisha whom I was around daily. She was about seventeen and she watched me often while my mother worked. We lived with her family for a few months.

I annoyed Keisha. She was forced to deal with me because she was the only other young girl in the household. So I often sat in her pissy bedroom watching *Matlock*, bored to death.

It must've been a Saturday morning when my life became eggless. No one was home, except me and Keisha. She listened to music on the radio as she made breakfast. I watched her and patiently waited for the food to be done as she loudly sang "Poison" by Bell Biv Devoe.

It's drivin' me out of my mind!

That's why it's hard for me to find

Can't get it out of my head!

Miss her, kiss her, love her

That girl is poison

Never trust a big butt and smile

That girl is poison

"How much longer?" I asked, abruptly interrupting her singing.

"Don't rush me. It will be done when I say it's done," she hissed, then continued singing with the spatula in her hand.

Ignoring her remarks, I asked, "What are you cooking? Can I just have cereal?"

"No. You will eat what I cook, little girl," she barked.

I saw her dip the bread into the bowl of eggs, which had brown stuff floating around in it. I yelled over the music, "Why are you putting bread in the eggs? My mother makes me bacon and toast, or potatoes. Do you have potatoes?"

She threw the remaining brown eggs into the pan. "Stop asking me all these dumb questions. Are you hungry or not? It's almost done."

An eternity later, she handed me a plate with brown eggs and one slice of bacon. "I only get one piece of bacon?" I immediately asked before the plate hit the table.

"You're an ungrateful little girl. You know that? Eat all those eggs too. You can't leave the table until your food is done," she demanded with a sneaky smirk on her face.

"Why didn't I get bread with eggs, like you?" I pouted. She ignored me and poured syrup on her French toast. She continued singing and bopping to the music.

The first bite of eggs traumatized me for life. She'd made my eggs with the leftover French toast batter. They tasted like cinnamon and salt. They were absolutely disgusting. I put the fork down and ate the one slice of bacon. She looked at me intensely, and I frowned every time I looked at the eggs.

"Hmm, my food is so good," she teased. "How is yours?"

"I don't think I like eggs. Can I have some cereal, please?"

"After all my hard work. You are going to eat those eggs. I'll sit right here with you until you are done."

There I sat with a fork and a plate full of French toast eggs that a pissy chick named Keisha was making me eat. I ate them all. I repeated this story in my mind my entire childhood. Whenever someone offered me eggs, I quickly told them, "No, thanks. I don't eat eggs." It was so strange because I noticed no one's eggs looked brown like hers, but I still repeated the story that eggs were disgusting.

I didn't try eggs again until I was about twelve years old. One of my friends assured me they were delicious. It was a bacon, egg, and cheese sandwich, and she was right. Eggs were actually good. Imagine all the potato salad, deviled eggs, breakfast sandwiches, scrambled eggs, and many other forms of cooked eggs I had missed out on because I repeated this story.

Triggers From Repeating An Old Story

WHAT TRIGGERS WERE A RESULT OF REPEATING THIS OLD STORY every time someone mentioned eggs? Let's break down my mind's thought process really quick.

- I hate eggs

- I hate cinnamon

- I hate people cooking for me

- I hate the smell of piss

- I hate finishing my food

- I think of eggs whenever I hear the song "Poison"

I then carried around the burden of avoiding eggs, all because of one incident that happened decades ago. I'm sure Keisha never replayed that story in her mind; it only existed at that moment for her. Keisha didn't wake up five years later and think, "I hate little girls because once I had to cook for a nagging four-year-old."

Now, instead of a simple story about eating brown eggs, imagine repeating a serious story like molestation, death, mental abuse, or physical abuse, and the impact it would have on your spirit. There were darker stories – I'm talking really dark – that I repeated in my mind, traumatizing me before I learned to let them go. It's all in my book, *DAMAGED little girl*.

If I had chosen to *become* those stories, I wouldn't be writing this book right now. I'd probably be in twenty-four-hour therapy. I know from personal experience how dropping a story can change your life for the better, and not just with eggs. Imagine all the other things you're missing out on by telling an old story that's no longer relevant.

In the game of life, your piece on the board can't move back; it can only move forward. Picture a game of chess. You made your move against your opponent, and it was a bad move. Your opponent is now making their move, and then it's your turn again. You make a new move which looks promising for your future moves. Six moves later, are you going to discuss a move you made five minutes ago, or are you going to keep moving forward? To discuss a move you made five minutes ago is not living! That moment has passed.

That is how you must look at the stories you repeat. They are the past.

Am I saying to never reminisce on the good times? Of course not! If it's a good memory and you are living in that moment with friends or family, that is still living in the moment. Bad memories need to be released to make space for new thoughts and new feelings. You should never feel proud of who you were ten years ago. What are you doing *now* that feels good? You should be your best self right now.

Create a new story. Easier said than done, right? No! I'm not taking it easy on you. I'm giving you the raw truth because I come with love. You can create a new story right this second. Decide right now who you want to be. Slow down, right now! Remember: You don't have to follow any of society's rules. What does the real you want to do?

Right now, take a moment to breathe in and slowly breathe out. Do it again. Breathe in and slowly breathe out. You are alive, Baby! So right this second, decide who you want to be. Are you a singer, a housewife, a chef, a dancer, a writer, a teacher, an entrepreneur, a hippie, a parent, a mentor, a coach, an inventor, a counselor? What makes you smile when you think of it? If you can't think of anything right now, it's ok. It will come to you from that little voice I told you to listen for.

If you are not sure who you want to be in your new story, think about who you **don't** want to be in your old story. Are you tired of working that sucky, unfulfilling job? Then start looking for a new one, not ten years from now, but right now. You are not guaranteed to be here ten years from now. Start living right now! Are you tired of being a full-time parent? Then find a hobby for yourself. No excuses! Use that beautiful brain of yours to figure it out. Are you tired of people-pleasing? Create a new *you* that pleases *you* first, and if you have energy left for others, then do so at that time.

Poor Victims

To all the victims, this is an open space and I will talk to you like I talk to my real friends. Get your shit together! Yup, I said it. Drop the "I'm a victim" attitude right here and now. Everyone has witnessed some type of trauma in their life, whether it was mental abuse, physical abuse, sexual abuse, or lack of love.

SUNNI T. CONNOR

Your trauma is not special, and your circumstances are not more severe than the little girl who dropped her candy on the ground, which in her reality was a huge tragedy. The reason your tragedy is not special is that no matter how hard life kicked your ass, your reaction was what made you the victim.

Victims love to explain how they had it so hard. They love to explain how their situation was worse than others' situations, as if this gives them the right to act in such negative ways. Also, being a victim usually comes with a lot of attention and sympathy.

The truth, though, is we all live in our own minds twenty-four-seven, so any difficulty we experience can send us into a deep depression, depending on how we react to life's circumstances. Here are two different examples.

The Single Mother

A SINGLE MOTHER OF THREE KIDS went to work late due to a flat tire. She was called into the office and was fired from her job. On her way home, she crashed her car, which she had just paid off after five years of payments. Now she has no car, no job, and three hungry children at home depending on her. She is hysterical and devastated. She feels life is always making everything hard for her. She's falling apart, and she considers giving up.

The Rich

ON THE OTHER SIDE OF TOWN, there is a housewife with three kids, too. She woke up to a mess on the floor and a screaming baby. Her husband hadn't returned home the night before. He stayed out with his mistress, yet again. Money is not an issue for them – they have plenty of it – but she doesn't work or do anything fulfilling for herself. She cooks, cleans, and serves her family all day. In her spare time, she medicates her disappointment with prescription drugs. She receives a call from her husband that he is leaving her for his mistress. She is hysterical and devastated, so much so that she contemplates suicide.

Who Deserves To Be A Victim?

WHICH WOMAN IS MORE OF A VICTIM? Who deserves sympathy more? Who deserves to give up on life or fall into a deep depression? In both of their minds, their situation is their reality. It's painful and it's what they have to face at the moment.

Let's continue to play out how each woman's life could be affected by their temporary circumstances.

The single mother wakes up the next day and decides, *"Forget that job! I have to feed my babies. I didn't like that job anyway, and that car needed a transmission so I was going to buy a new car soon anyway. I'll just go out with my girls and have a drink. I'll start job hunting tomorrow."* She had a rough day, she cried herself to sleep, and she woke up in action mode. She didn't blame God, life, the car, poverty, or society for her bad day. She felt the pain at that moment and made her next move on the chess board.

The housewife wakes up the next morning and pops some pills and lies in a dark room, alone and depressed. She later calls her mother and all her friends and repeats the story over and over until everyone in her contact list knows what her cheating husband has done to her. Two months went by and she is still lying around, sad and convinced she's a victim. Every new person she meets, she makes sure to tell them she is getting a divorce, and she explains how awful her life is. She has become victimized. She doesn't come up with an action plan to get her life back on track, and even two years after the divorce, it's still the first thing she tells people.

She never made her next move on the chess board; she stayed stuck because she didn't know how to gain the courage to make her next move. She became a victim.

Everyone handles emotions differently in their minds. What's small to you may be huge to someone else. No matter how you perceive your pain or trauma, though, you must accept them and move on. This is the only road to true happiness. Stop telling the sad story. We all have one. Instead of being a victim, decide to learn the game so you have no hesitation on your next move. Yes, her sorry-ass husband left her. He wasn't the man for her if he was staying out with another woman, anyway. She deserved better, but she ignored his infidelity until life forced her to learn the hard way. Had she stopped being a victim, she would've known it was a blessing that her husband left her. Had she stopped telling the same sad story, she could've started healing and found the love of her life. Instead, she turned bitter.

How Do You Go From Being A Victim To Being A Conqueror?

EVERY VICTIM'S FIRST APPROACH TO PAIN MUST BE TO LEARN. I know it's easier to blame the abuser, but you must find the lesson in the pain. It's there, trust me. I understand it was the abuser who took something from you or hurt you. But that doesn't change the fact that you must find the lesson if you want to properly make your next move.

There are three very important questions I want you to ask yourself before you run to family and friends to hear advice or to vent.

1. What role did I play in what happened?

2. What did I learn from this situation?

3. How can I avoid repeating this kind of pain/trauma?

There are many situations where a true victim is at the wrong place at the wrong time, or a child gets hurt by an adult, by no means am I saying there are no true victims. Nor, am I saying your pain is not valid.

Before I can speak about how to go from being a victim to being a conqueror, I must address people's childhood pain. This may sound harsh, so be prepared.

Whatever happened in your childhood, no matter how awful, brutal, degrading, traumatizing, or unfair—you have to let it go! You are torturing yourself! We are only here in the game of life for a short period of time to experience life, and we don't get years to waste on trauma. Truth is, the pain you are still experiencing from a childhood tragedy is the pain you are causing yourself. It's the old story you refuse to let go of. The abuser has moved on, yet you still allow them to control your inner power. I am speaking from my own experience, from the many traumatic events I suffered as a child. I'm only the person I am today because I chose to create a new story.

As long as you have that old victim story, you will excuse your actions. It's the reason you tell yourself why you are so screwed up. The hard truth is, you are so screwed up because you take yourself back to that painful childhood repeatedly and live in a moment from the past which has nothing to do with your current reality.

I don't think a psychologist or a therapist will be too happy with my approach to people's traumas. They may even advise against reading advice like this. The truth hurts. Every word in this book is drawn from difficult experiences I faced in my own life—until, that is, I learned the power of aligning myself with the universe, which resulted in me leaving the pack of society's followers.

To go from victim to conqueror, you must first acknowledge that something happened to you. Then figure out why it happened. Own it. Even if you feel it wasn't your fault, still own it. When I say own it, I'm not saying you raped yourself, or that it was your fault in any way. Nor am I saying you gave yourself black eyes, or that it was your fault your father beat you as a kid, or that you're to blame for your mother's decision to leave you home alone your entire childhood. Instead, I'm saying, "Own that those things actually happened to you."

Next, you have to forgive. I want you to forgive the other person, and the situation, and then forgive yourself. It's the only way you can free your mind and release negativity. It's your gateway to happiness.

Finally, conquer the pain. You may have to repeat these steps multiple times until you let go, but keep letting go. One day that old story will no longer have relevance.

Pain

I'M VERY FAMILIAR WITH PAIN. It can feel so heavy and overwhelming. I often felt like I was carrying heavy weights on my heart. Mental or physical pain can take over your experience, if you let it. I know this because I have allowed mental pain to suck the joy right out of my being. I've been so hurt that I've watched the real me fade away while a bitter version of me took over. It took time before I recognized the bitter chick wasn't really me.

Look at mental pain as a very temporary emotion. I want you to put mental pain in a category with happy, sad, scared, or other emotions you feel throughout the day. Not in the sense that pain will come to you every day, but in the sense that pain doesn't have a special place to sit and dwell in your heart. Happiness does not have a permanent place in your heart. Being happy is a temporary emotion that you feel at the moment something makes you happy. Treat pain the same way. The moment something or someone causes you pain, deal with it at that moment. Don't hold onto it for years to come. There will be new pain from a new story, so let the old pain and the old story go.

Releasing mental pain is not easy. Our minds naturally stay consumed with past experiences and obsess over future experiences that we haven't encountered yet. This behavior is a huge problem, and it's responsible for most of our mental pain.

For example:

You and your significant other have a big fight in the morning about spending more time together.

That entire day, your mind replays the fight and the hurtful things you said to one another. Then your mind starts thinking about the future and how you two might not be together. That thought alone causes you great pain. Those images of separation start playing in your mind before anything has actually occurred.

Two days pass, and you and your partner still aren't talking. Now your mind has built up momentum on the subject of spending time together. It tells you how many nights you are lonely and how someone who really loves you would sacrifice to be with you. The thoughts continue in a downward pattern.

The real truth is that the fight with your significant other happened days ago. That pain is over. You kept that pain alive by reliving the story. Your mind loves to keep stories alive, and it also loves to predict what terrible things will happen in the future. The mind is literally insane.

There's a simple but hard solution to mental pain: You have to get in the now. There is no pain in the now. Only your mind can take you to the past or predict the future, but at this moment there is no pain. So if you can quiet your mind and find the now, instead of focusing on a fight you had days ago, you can make a decision in the current moment to find extra time for the both of you. You won't dwell on what happened.

You may have noticed that I said the solution to mental pain was both simple and hard. That's because one of the hardest things for people to do is to stay in the current moment. The mind takes over and tries to keep you in problem-solving mode. That is the illusion. There actually aren't any problems in the now. Most issues happened days ago, and you've already found a solution. You can't let the pain in the mind win. Use your mind as a tool. When it starts rambling nonsense, try to find the now. The current moment will shut that noise up every time. To win the game of life while you are alive, you must consciously get into the now.

Pain can also be good. We feel some form of pain to protect us as well. Why do you think our bodies hurt if we do something painful to ourselves? It's to keep us from self-destructing. If we could cut off a pinky toe and feel nothing, I'm sure some people would break their own fingers out of anger, but they don't do so because they know it will be painful.

Pain also makes us level up. When pain hurts, you remember it. You never want to feel that pain again, so you make better decisions.

Another way to release old pain that you've been carrying for years is to teach others from your own experiences. Help someone who was in an abusive relationship, teach someone how to overcome addiction, show someone how to gain self-esteem, and do your part in the game. Don't fall victim to the many circumstances, but instead conquer them, make your next move, find the now, and help the player behind you.

4

Everything Is A Choice

"*You have the choice to create the life your heart is yearning to live.*"

~Mahatma Gandhi

Don't Let Society Make Your Choices

EVERYTHING IS A CHOICE, so don't you dare let society choose for you. You always know the answer to any question. Some solutions just may be harder to accomplish, which is why we like to ask people for advice. We already know the choice we need to make, but we love to ask others in the hopes they will give us an easier answer. Let me tell you something about advice: It's good for making conversation, but not much else. You must always consult with yourself first. I think it's time for an analogy before we get too deep into this chapter.

There was a woman whose boyfriend beat her every day. They had two little girls together. The woman was afraid of her boyfriend. She felt trapped because she hadn't finished school or completed any of her career goals. He was the breadwinner, and she had no education or source of income.

One day, her boyfriend came home angry and smacked one of the little girls. The woman tried to help her daughter and walked right into a mighty punch, which caused two of her teeth to go flying out of her mouth. The woman screamed out of anger and hit her mate with a frying pan. She was tired of not defending herself. She looked at him lying flat on the floor with no movement or emotion on his face. Her daughter called the police. The police arrived and announced her boyfriend dead on the scene. She was arrested. She went to jail telling her victim story of how she was in an abusive relationship for over ten years, and how no one helped her and now she must serve time for finally defending herself.

This is a tough situation. Can we agree? There are many ways this story could've played out. There is one fact, though, and I want you to really absorb it: SHE HAD A CHOICE. We are not going to debate if she had an easy or hard choice. We are just simply acknowledging that she had a choice. She could've left the relationship years ago and got her kids to safety, gone back to school, started a business, started a foundation to prevent the abuse of women, or whatever she wanted to do.

She could've stopped being the victim and left. We are all aware these situations can be dangerous, but that doesn't change the fact that she had a choice. She could have left the first time he smacked her, long before she even conceived children with him. Every day was a choice to stay there. Every day was a choice to forgive him for the last beating.

Let's discuss the death of the boyfriend. She still had a choice up until the end of his life. She chose to hit him with the frying pan, she chose not to run, and she chose to defend herself.

This analogy was not used for judgment; it was used to show that we have choices the entire time we have breath in our bodies. I chose to start working on this chapter today so I can stay on schedule. I chose to eat fast food because I was too busy today to prepare a healthy meal, and now my tummy is rolled over my pants and I feel disgusting. I chose to wake up at four-thirty this morning instead of sleeping in. I chose to tell you about my day right now! You chose to keep reading. No matter how big or how small, we have choices all day long. Don't let society or anyone else make your choices for you. You can take your family's and friends' advice and use the parts that make sense, but you must make your own choices and live with them.

——*ell*——

STORYTIME

"I almost cared"

Can we get a little personal?

I struggled with the transparency I decided to put in this book. This included the choice to discuss religion, race, and other controversial topics throughout the chapters. I was also advised not to use profanity because it can bring the quality of the writing down. This advice was coming from a good friend with no ill intentions. Our conversation went like this.

"Why shouldn't I use profanity throughout the chapters?" I asked with a curious look.

"People won't like it, and it may come off as bad writing. People are critical and they appreciate traditional literature, especially non-fiction."

"What people?" I politely asked.

"The people who will read the book, silly," she said in a joking tone.

"Oh, so I should write what people will accept so I can sell more books?" I asked.

"Yes." She frowned with confusion before continuing, "What about people who don't understand your concepts? Should you mention God and the universe so much? And what about you calling religion control? Some will surely hate you for that. Not to mention, you kind of said African American is not a race. Are you crazy? That could be offensive."

"So I shouldn't write what I believe, in order to please society? Now *that* sounds crazy!" I barked back.

"It's a better way to do it. You want to reach a larger audience, right?"

"Of course. I want to share this book with as many people as possible."

"So you have to write to please the majority." She continued on and on like a nagging grandmother.

I glanced back at my keyboard and continued typing before responding. "But I made a choice," I firmly responded.

"Is it the right choice?" she asked with big bright eyes.

I raised my head. "Good question, but the answer is irrelevant because it's *my choice.*"

"So that means you don't care how people will take your work?"

"No, what it means is I will write what I want! I will sell millions to those who can accept it, and for those who can't, it wasn't for them because I don't live for society. My readers will love it, and when they finish reading, they will know which version of themselves is running the show."

This is the exact conversation I had with my dear friend. My dear friend was, "ME!" I had choices to make about this book, and before calling every contact in my phone, I talked to myself and decided to write with pure passion and authenticity. Have you realized I'm crazy yet? What is normal, anyway? Who wants to live a mediocre life when you can have a life filled with adventure? Who wants to actually follow the rules? I'm yawning just thinking about it.

Your Inner Being

As I STRESS THROUGHOUT THIS BOOK, there's a big reason why you have to find that special voice. Your inner being helps you with your decisions, and even when you screw up, your inner being doesn't care. Your inner spirit came here with you, and you could do no wrong. It's only the ego that tears us apart. So no matter what choices you make, live with them and prepare to make your next move. Don't let guilt or doubt hold you too long in a decision. Make a choice and stick with it. Don't let others choose anything for you! Ever! You can take in what they advise, but don't you dare take in their choices.

They Are Just Followers

REMEMBER, MOST PEOPLE HAVE NO IDEA WHAT THE HELL THEY ARE DOING HERE. The majority are following. Why do you think social media calls people "followers"? That's what the masses do. They follow. If one person does a social media challenge, here come the other millions of people who are influenced and want to fit in. People crave acceptance, which ironically causes them a great deal of unhappiness.

If you made it this far in the book, we now personally know each other. You know a bit about me, and I know you want to stop standing in line with the other robots. I won't disappoint you. Don't disappoint me.

Finish this book and you will laugh at the others, not in a judgmental way but in a way that says, "I can't believe I used to be just like that!"

How To Handle Bad Choice

HOW DO YOU HANDLE A BAD CHOICE? Fuck it! Okay, I'm sorry. Actually, I'm not sorry! I'm still going to go with "Fuck it." Do you know why? What can you really do about it? I mean, seriously, what can you do? You can make the next choice better to help fix the wrong one. But that original bad choice is gone; it was already made. We move forward on the game board, remember? So, what's the next move?

Every minute in life is like a restart button. We just have to slow down long enough to absorb what happened, and it will be okay. We are still alive and we can keep going. Just breathe and restart.

Bad choices are not actually bad. We are here to experience life, and decisions are a huge part of the experience. We get lessons from the choices we make, and they ultimately mold the people we become. We are entirely too hard on ourselves! According to researchers, we have to make about thirty-five thousand choices per day. I did a little research on my own mind, and I discovered I had to make a choice every few seconds. I made very simple choices throughout the day. For the heck of it, let's go over a few choices I made within a few moments of waking up. Come join me in my mind really quickly.

- Ugh, those emails are waiting, should I just stop daydreaming and answer the emails now? *(Nope, I'll go make my tea first.)*

- Do I feel like cutting up ginger for my tea? *(Nope, I'll just use the honey.)*

- School conferences are this week. Should I do Thursday or Friday? *(Friday it is!)*

- My car needs an oil change *(Not today)*

- Smoothie, or shrimp and grits? *(I have a busy day. Grits will hold me longer.)*

I had to make all these simple choices within the first few minutes of opening my eyes this morning. Now, what if I overly judged myself or was hard on myself for making one wrong choice today? How stupid would that be when there is another choice waiting just around the corner? I want you to look at choices as if they mean nothing, as if they are a dime a dozen. So what if you miscalculated one of your choices? Now's your chance to make a better choice.

Wealthy people have a very special technique for choices. They make them quickly and change them slowly. They don't dwell on the possibility of making the wrong choice. As long as you are breathing, it will be okay.

Let's slow down for a quick second. Take your index finger, put it under your nose, and lightly blow. Did you feel the wind of your breath? You are here! You exist! No one is bigger than you. You have an abundance of life in your body just like other humans. Don't waste time being indecisive or overthinking. Be bold. Be confident. Be curious. Make your choices without regret.

Living With A Bad Choice

OKAY, SO YOU SCREWED UP AND YOU MADE A BAD CHOICE. Now what? Let's just use one of my choices from this morning as an example. Let's go with the

"My car needs an oil change" choice. I said "Screw that car" this morning because I chose to use my time in another manner. But let's imagine I have an important meeting later, and the engine blows up in the middle of the day because the oil is so filthy and low. I procrastinated too long and now the car is junk. What's the first thing I have to do? I have to make a new choice.

- Will I beat myself up for not getting an oil change, and miss the meeting?

- Will I sit here and call a friend to complain?

- Will I waste time and get the car towed?

- Will I catch an Uber to the meeting and leave the piece of crap on the side of the road?

- Will I call the clients and inform them I'm running late?

- Will I call a family member for help?

I personally would've left the car on the side of the road and made my important meeting. It's not like the car was going anywhere. Forget about the original bad choice of "Not getting the oil change." There is always another choice waiting around the corner. Make a sound choice and move on.

Emotions

FIRST, FEEL HOW YOU FEEL! There will always be plenty of people around you who try to tell you how to feel, but screw that. Feel how you feel in every moment, acknowledge it, and let it pass. Society will actually make you feel like you are weak for crying, or try to convince you that you are unlikeable for being angry. Emotions are part of the human experience. They're our guidance system, helping us understand what we do and don't want.

Anger is an emotion I felt just today. Something pissed me off. Others stared judgmentally at me as if I was overreacting, but I wasn't because that's how I felt on the inside. Once I calmed down, I went right back to my happy place. But it felt great to scream, "Fuck!" It's better to release the anger than walk around bitter every day because you want to look like you're too tough for anything to affect you.

Sadness is an underrated emotion. There is power in releasing tears. Finally letting go of the burden in your heart actually changes you as a person. Releasing the pain or the sadness from within allows you freedom.

Brief Intermission

MEN, I WANT TO DIRECT THIS STATEMENT JUST TO YOU. It's okay to cry. It's okay to show emotion. You are human too and we love you. You are beautiful creatures who deserve to release emotions just like everyone else. If you are not comfortable crying in front of others, go to the bathroom and let it out, because we need you. We need the highest versions of our men. Release and move forward. I know it's a lot of pressure on men to be strong, fearless, and emotionless. Society fed you that narrative. But you can change that by choosing the real you and giving yourself permission to feel how you feel. I love you, and there are so many women depending on you, and we are fighting for your mental health. Don't be a threat to yourself. Choose your well-being, and just know there are millions of us rooting for you. We are waiting for you to BECOME.

Okay, Back To Emotions

I WON'T SPEAK ON ALL THE EMOTIONS LIKE FEAR, SHAME, AND GUILT because they come up throughout other chapters in this book. I will, however, speak about happiness. I've talked to people over the years and I've asked them, "What is the one thing you want out of life?" The most common answer was, "I just want to be happy!" That always confused me. People speak of being happy like it's a permanent state. Happiness is a temporary emotion, just like sadness. No one is happy all the time, nor are they sad all the time. When you feel happiness, indulge in it! Really feel it. Don't chase happiness as a goal for your life; just enjoy it when it shows up. You can choose to be happy more than you choose to be angry or sad. That's a choice, but it's still not a permanent state. Nothing here is permanent. This entire illusion is temporary, and so are your emotions.

We often choose to keep our emotions bottled up. Let it out. It will release stuck energy, which will allow you to keep being great. Just because I said to let it out, though, that doesn't mean you have to share it with everyone. I used to share all my feelings, but I'm slowly learning to keep things to myself. I don't have to say everything out loud. Someone dear to me constantly reminded me of things I said when I was emotional. I knew emotions were temporary, but that person took my words for face value. That's when I realized I shouldn't overly share my emotions, and I should learn to control my emotions until I got into a sacred place.

I've said some hurtful things while I was in an angry state. They were not my true feelings; I was acting on my emotions. That's okay. I made a bad choice. I didn't have to keep living with that bad choice, though, so I accepted it and let it go. People often get stuck in life by perceiving reality as a final outcome. It's not. You can change your reality anytime you want with the power of intention. You can make a new choice in a matter of seconds.

We only get a little bit of time in this vibrational universe, and we can't waste any of it dwelling on our mistakes. We were designed to make mistakes—it's what makes life so grand. How much fun would a perfect life be? If we were all perfect, then why would we create? If life was already perfect, there would be nothing for us to do here. What would there be to experience? There's no time to dwell on what or how we did things. Learn from your mistakes and make a better choice next time.

5

Thoughts

"*Nothing can harm you as much as your own thoughts unguarded.*"

~ Buddha

How Our Minds Process Thoughts

I WANT TO SHOW YOU HOW YOUR MIND WORKS, so you can recognize who you are and who you are **not**. You must control your mind and watch the "judger." The judger is the part of your brain that judges everything you do. The judger feels guilt, revenge, hate, and every other emotion that is not your true self. Your true self would never feel those emotions about you because all your soul wants is what's best for you, just as your body only wants to keep you alive.

There are four types of thoughts I want to discuss.

Random Thoughts

THESE ARE VALUELESS THOUGHTS accumulated from things you've heard while living in society.

Example of Random Thoughts:

"I should've washed clothes before reading this book." "Did I water the plants yesterday?" "Should I cook or go out for dinner?" "Should I wear dark colors today?" "No one liked any of my Instagram posts that I put up twenty minutes ago." "I'm bored."

There is not a human on this planet right now that doesn't have random thoughts. To truly control your mind, you have to start by recognizing which thoughts are *yours* and which thoughts are a combination of all of our thoughts as a collective. If we are energy and there are billions of us, that would mean there are many energetic thoughts that we bounce off each other. That's good news, because it means you can stop taking your thoughts so seriously. Especially knowing they are not all yours. It's also bad news because if you are not aware, you will take societal thoughts to be true.

Where does society fit in this equation? Society is part of our random thoughts. We have so much unnecessary information stored in our minds about what others think. They are statements we heard at one time or another that emotionally affected us, so we stored the thoughts. Some of these beliefs were introduced to us at a very young age. Random thoughts come in and out. The less attention you pay them, the more your mind will look for more stimulating thoughts.

Why am I talking about random or pointless thoughts? Because I want you to be able to study your mind. I want you to be aware that you are a GOD to your body. You are running this show. You have to know what's worth your effort and what to ignore. Someone's opinion about you is like a random thought. It means nothing. Just because the mass of us agree on certain topics doesn't mean we're right. I think we all agree the color green is green. Enough of us agreed that it's okay to call that color green. It doesn't mean it's factual. If a group of birds flew over acres of land, I seriously doubt one of them would call the grass "green" or even call it "grass" for that matter. They are on this planet, too, but maybe they don't agree that green is green. So is it a fact?

We don't have to follow the masses, and listening to random thoughts is doing just that. Now, I will admit that agreeing on certain things makes life easier. It makes it easier for us to communicate if we agree on the simple principles of life. Being against violence, child pornography, and so on as a society benefits all of us. I'm not against humanity and how far we've come to make this planet a magical place. I am against you not knowing your true self and how to separate from the pack to live your own experience.

Focused Thoughts

FOCUSED THOUGHTS ARE THOUGHTS you are intentionally thinking to accomplish a goal.

Example of Focused Thoughts:

"I need to finish writing that chapter." "I have to email my business partner the new financial report." "Today I will pick out the fabric for my new clothing line." "I'll pay all the bills before I start spending this weekend."

Focused thoughts, on the other hand, can be very beneficial. You can use focused thoughts to manifest things you want in your reality.

There is a small problem with focused thoughts, though: They are not open to the impossible. You can become so focused that you think you have all the answers, which shuts out the power of the universe. We must always be open to the impossible, because that's where the true magic lies. I'm focused right now as I'm typing these words. However, I'm also aligned with a force higher than myself, which is allowing the words to flow more freely.

Here's how I'm using my focused thoughts at this very moment. I focused on my intention for this chapter, I focused on the title of this chapter, and I focused on the computer screen to ensure my thoughts were correctly appearing in front of me. Am I focused on the next sentence? NO! I am letting thoughts flow to me, which in turn are flowing to you at this moment.

A good time for focused thoughts is when you are taking a test, interviewing for a job, having blood drawn, driving serious machinery, or doing anything else that requires your focus. Even with those things, you still need your higher self. It's your intuition that will answer all the questions on a test that you forgot when you were studying. It's your higher self that will allow your personality to show up during a job interview instead of being a stiff-focused board. It's your higher self that whispers in your ear that another car is turning at the same time you are, which helps you avoid an accident. So even with focus, you need your higher self, your true self.

Negative Thoughts

NEGATIVE THOUGHTS ARE THOUGHTS you think to sabotage yourself or others.

Example of Negative Thoughts:

"I'm a horrible mom. I never do things the right way. Every time I try to be better, I just let everyone down. Everyone is not meant to be a mother, and surely that includes me." "Why am I even here, when all I do is screw things up? My mother always said I wouldn't be worth anything. She must be right." "I really shouldn't have eaten that cake. I'm already overweight. That's probably why my husband keeps cheating on me. Look at my stomach sticking out over my pants—I'm sure everyone can see it. Why do people have cake at parties like this anyway, just so I can become fatter? Look at her walking by, looking all skinny. I looked like that ten years ago, before I had children with my cheating husband. I won't eat anything else at this party."

Negative thoughts, I believe, are the reason the mind experiences temporary stages of insanity. What person in their right mind would beat themselves down with harsh thoughts seventy to eighty percent of the day? It can't really be *you*. Would the real *you* sabotage yourself all day long? Would the real you feel guilty for something you did ten years ago? Do you think the universe is upset with you for something you did so long ago?

Is it possible that the only thing that really matters is this moment? God is too busy creating worlds to keep tabs on something you did ten years ago, something that allowed you to learn a lesson to help you become who you are right now. Everything is a lesson, and there is no higher power faulting you for learning. It would be like a kid in kindergarten forgetting some letters in the alphabet, and the teacher punishing the child for trying to learn them again. Anything wrong you did, you weren't capable of doing better at that moment. But you now know better and that moment is gone. You are the only one holding that grudge against self. I've done this to myself, but I now know the version I am today wouldn't consciously make those mistakes, because I learned from them in the past. We are constantly learning. To solve the negative thoughts that pop into your mind all day, you first must acknowledge them and realize they are not your thoughts.

If you find yourself thinking negative thoughts a lot throughout the day, I want you to start listening to what the thoughts are saying. Don't listen to defend yourself or to respond. Just listen. If the negative thought is saying something that you truly want to change about yourself – your weight, for example – then use that thought as motivation. Get up and take a walk. Shut the thought up. Eat a little less at dinner. Shut the thought up.

This is a balanced universe, and you can always use evil to create good. There are good and bad here on this planet, and no one is immune to both sides of this experience. But you are creating your own reality, and you can choose what to do with your thoughts.

Now, what if a negative thought has no purpose, like criticizing something you can't change? Your race, for example. Then you know for a fact that the negative thought is coming from an outside source. You know you picked thoughts up from someone else's opinion or things you heard from society. You can laugh at those thoughts because they are irrelevant. But you must slow down long enough to acknowledge that those kinds of thoughts are from an outside influence. Clearly the real you wouldn't complain about your race. You were born that race and your spirit jumped into your body as that race. Why would the real you ever judge that? Those negative thoughts have no purpose, and they are wasting space in your mind.

Universal Thoughts

UNIVERSAL THOUGHTS ARE THOUGHTS that flow to you very quietly and without force. They feel good and it takes no effort to follow them.

Example of Universal Thoughts:

"I think I'll light a candle and take a hot bath. Yes, that will feel good." "I feel good today, so maybe I'll invest in that stock I was thinking about." "I'm so excited to write the next chapter of my book." "I miss my friends. I always laugh with them, so let me see if they can come out tonight." "I think I'll go for a walk after dinner—the weather is so nice." "I'm grateful for everything I have."

Yay!!!! My favorite thoughts of all. It makes me so excited to talk about the magical thoughts that create worlds. I don't like saying magical too much, because some people interpret the word magical as airy, fairy, or fake shit. I'm not using the word in the sense of a magic trick, but rather in the sense of what's in the imagination, what's unseen or unknown. Universal thoughts are never forced. They follow the path of least resistance. There is no judgment, only what feels good at that moment. Being happy is not a one-time thing. Being happy is choosing the best thoughts, energies, and vibrations in the current moment. All we truly have is this moment right now, so this is the only moment you truly have to be happy.

Can we stop and acknowledge for a moment that we are in a universe? Think about how small our problems are compared to being on a planet that's spinning perfectly, with the right amount of abundance to keep it going. You have that same power in you. You can keep going! Don't let life or your thoughts make you think you are not worthy. If you are alive, you are worthy of any and everything that exists in this time and space.

How do I know this? I know this because we are energy and everything is vibrating, so if you weren't worthy of being part of this energy and this vibration, you wouldn't be aligned to be on this planet at this time. Maybe your time would've been in the past, or perhaps you would have come here in the future. But, nope, you are here right now, so you are a part of all that is right now. You are not exempt from this special place, but you have to start perceiving it for what it really is. Life is the opportunity to experience this journey however you want with unlimited possibilities.

Thoughts really do become things, especially universal thoughts. There are many ways we can tap into the unlimited possibilities. We can allow our thoughts to create our reality, or we can create our own reality with intentional/universal thoughts. The universe will do the rest. The work is not yours to be done alone. Don't think your thoughts can do it all.

Three Steps To Manifesting With Thoughts

HERE ARE THREE THINGS I WANT YOU TO DO when you are ready to manifest something with a universal thought.

1. Think about exactly what you want without allowing doubt. Don't put any pressure on the thought. Just think about what you want. Fall into a daydream of how your life will feel with that thing. If any negative thoughts pop up, laugh at them and say you are not the *true*

me, because the *true me* wants this beautiful thing.

2. Immediately believe you can have it. Don't come up with all the ways you can't have it. Think of all the ways you deserve to have it. Thank the universe in advance for giving it to you.

3. Lastly, feel good about what you are about to receive. That will be your motivation for action. Start right away, while it feels good.

———ele———

STORYTIME

"DAMAGED little girl"

So here's a true story of how I applied the three methods above with intentional and universal thoughts. I intentionally thought about how I wanted to publish my first book. I knew I had to tell my story and I knew people would be motivated by reading what I had overcome. I didn't doubt my ability to write, but I feared how others would feel about me speaking my truth. When you are telling your life story, unfortunately, you have to include others because you don't live your life alone. I knew my story was rough and I knew everyone involved wasn't ready to expose the skeletons in their closets. But I felt it was my only way to release all that had happened to me. So I decided to tell the world, and I became obsessed with my manuscript.

First, I knew exactly what I wanted. I wanted to publish my own book and keep all the rights because I knew in the future I might want to make it into a movie. I daydreamed of people reading my book all over the world. I wanted every prison in the US to have *DAMAGED little girl* and I constantly told myself it was possible. When negative thoughts popped into my mind like, *"Girl, there are a million other books on the market. Why would they buy yours? How are you going to market something you never did before? Just using social media won't work. Who wants to hear your story?"* I laughed and said, *"Shut up, ego! I got this! Be cool and watch me work!"* The negative thoughts lost their power to the higher thoughts every time, and so they left.

Next, I immediately believed I could do it. So many others had done it, and I knew that if they could, so could I. I refused to let doubt control me. Nothing was going to stop me. I thought of all the ways I could succeed. All the ways it could work. I knew that my story was rare, that it was worth telling, and that it could help people. I knew I was a writer because I had been writing since elementary school. So there was no room for doubt.

Lastly, I felt good about it. I got excited every time I talked about it. I started thanking the universe every day for my first book before it even manifested. I said the name of it any chance I got in order to speak it into existence: "*DAMAGED little girl* this and *DAMAGED little girl* that!"

Now I had to start some action. I started by writing and researching. I had to learn how to format a book, publish a book, find an editor, fire many editors, find someone to create the cover I had envisioned in my mind, market the book, figure out how to get it in prisons and the list goes on and on and on. There were many steps I had to take to bring *DAMAGED little girl* into existence, but what started as an idea is now a full-fleshed book thousands of people have read. It's entered almost every prison in the US, been translated into Spanish (*Niña Dañada*), and sold copies in multiple countries.

That book was a universal thought: a calling, a passion, something my higher self enjoyed writing and sharing. Writing this book was also a universal thought, and there are so many more examples I could name. We can manifest all of our dreams if we can control our insane minds. We have to line up with what we want, believe it, and take action.

The truth is that your random and negative thoughts want to run your life. The majority of your thoughts are not conducive to the life you want to live. I often call the mind the enemy. What a disturbing hater the mind is. You say you can do this, it says you can't and then gives you every reason in the world to back up its argument. Would a thought that's aligned with who you really are be so focused on sabotaging you all day? What kind of person would choose to be negative against their own self? Most of us, that's who! Think about how insane that is. It's almost like chewing your own arm off or eating a piece of finger for dinner. You wouldn't destroy the body in that manner because you know it's a part of you. You wouldn't deliberately hurt part of yourself in that destructive way. So if you, the *real* you, wouldn't want to hurt yourself, then you must know those crazy thoughts are not *you*. This realization is the beginning of taking your mind back. It's where your freedom starts.

Problems Aren't Really Problems

Our minds actually create problems so they can solve them. One way to stop this nonsense in your mind is to avoid boredom. When you get bored, your thoughts go on a mission to satisfy your boredom. Mission one is usually to create a problem so that you can have something to solve. Rarely, though, can you solve it from that place of negative vibration. The problem and the solution are on two different frequencies. The solution is usually found within universal thoughts, when you are grounded and calm. The problem energy, on the other hand, is upset, angry, and solely focused on negativity. It can't find the solution while it's on such a low vibration.

Why would your mind create its own problems? Because it's bored. It doesn't want to be left alone. Your mind is constantly trying to keep a certain version of you alive so that the program can stay alive, but that version is not you.

How can you know what thoughts are really you? Only the ones that feel good. Yup, it's that simple. Your spirit that came here with you ONLY has your best interests in mind, and it believes in you more than your own mother does. Your spirit wants you to win the game, and it's constantly trying to remind you who you are. The other thoughts are a collection of memories, moments, societal influences, stereotypes, and so on. Learn to laugh at the foolery and watch it go away. Once the thoughts know you can separate the two, they will come less and less often. Since you don't give them energy anymore, they have no place in your mind. Problems become almost non-existent.

Have you ever seen those people who always look at life in a positive light? They are usually pretty annoying to most of us. You want them to take your problem seriously, but they just say something like, "everything will work itself out—it always does." They never quite give you the negative reaction you're looking for. It's because they've learned the secret. They've learned how not to take this place so seriously. They've also learned how to live life with more light and less darkness.

Your negative thoughts are darkness, and your true self is light. Choose the light. This takes practice. We are said to have more than 60,000 thoughts per day, and we process about 70,000 thoughts per day. Studies have shown that 70-80% of those thoughts are negative. You will have to practice controlling your thoughts. The negative thoughts won't completely go away, but with some focus that 70-80% can drop to 20% easily. Your life will change drastically when you take back your power.

Sometimes you can think of problems before they even happen. Like, "Next month I have to pay the electricity bill." Is next month here yet? Doesn't the bill always get paid? Doesn't God always make a way?

I'll end this chapter here with this final message: Don't let thoughts stress you out! Don't think too far into the future, unless you are thinking about positive things you want to manifest. Don't keep thinking about the past, either, unless you're focusing on good memories. Otherwise, bring yourself to the now. The now is where you are ageless and free of obsessive thoughts. You just are...

6

What Is Your Purpose?

"*The mystery of human existence lies not in just staying alive, but in finding something to live for.*"

~ Fyodor Dostoyevsky

Why Are We Here?

Who really knows? Maybe to experience or to evolve the planet. Maybe just to have fun and to learn. The reason we are here is not as important as what we can do while we are here. I believe we are here to create. We are here to contribute our gifts and skills to create a better experience for those who are coming after us. I don't have any facts to back that supposition up, but what I do know is the creativity of the people before us helped make this life experience enjoyable for us. Think about the first person who created a broom. How do you suppose people got the trash up before he/she invented a broom?

What about the way cars have been upgraded to mini-machines? Imagine walking to work every morning. Imagine walking to get groceries. I could go on and on about how the previous souls blessed us with the ability to live better. That is your purpose, too! You are not exempt from giving back to life. You don't get to sit around and watch the television that someone else created, eat the food someone else grew, use the soap someone else researched ingredients to make, ride in cars, fly on planes, or talk on a cell phone, all without contributing any effort of your own.

You are here to create as well. Get to it! Every one of us came here with a gift with which to bless life, and that gift must remain here when we leave, which means there will always be a piece of us here. I'm looking forward to seeing your gift. Some of us leave music behind for others to enjoy. Music is universal and eternal. It touches souls far beyond the artist's life span. I just listened to Michael Jackson this morning and felt every beat of the tune. Mike is no longer here, but his gift remains. Just like my books will remain part of this experience when I am gone. Everyone is not an inventor, singer, or writer; some of us are just here to make a change.

Did Dr. Martin Luther King Jr. invent anything, or have a platinum record? Did he make a table? Did he create a spaceship? No! He created change for the new generations that were to come. He left his mark here on the planet; he came here and he let his desires be known. That is your job, too. You came to this planet, so now let it be known.

What about Dick Gregory? He didn't invent anything, but he changed the mindset of millions by making them laugh and teaching them how to think differently and eat differently. I've had people tell me they don't have a purpose, they are just here. None of us are just here.

Why You Can't Find Your Purpose

IN MOST CASES, YOU CAN'T FIND YOUR PURPOSE FOR ONE OR MORE OF THE FOLLOWING REASONS.

1. You care what society will think of you if you live in your purpose.

2. You are living for others.

3. You are afraid of your true calling.

4. You are not connected to your inner being/soul.

5. You think your skill/gift won't make you money.

None of the above reasons is worth forfeiting an opportunity to live your life's purpose. Imagine if you could do whatever you want and feel however you want without the pressure of judgment. Do you think you would be able to see and feel more clearly? Every time you focus on what another person thinks, you take time away from your true desires.

Our time is limited, and every waking moment you have to remind yourself that you are here for a purpose. Some people get discouraged, thinking they have just one special purpose. That can be intimidating. I'm here to tell you, **your very existence is a purpose.** The circle of life includes you, and while you are here you are just as important as the sky, the grass, the trees, the celebrities, the politicians, etc. We share this space together to make magic.

Simply put, we are here to leave our gift for the upcoming generations.

How To Find Your Purpose

WHAT DOES SOCIETY HAVE TO DO WITH YOUR PURPOSE? What if I told you that the main reason you are not living your dreams is because of society? See, society tends to make rules about how everything should happen based on what others have done. What people don't tell you is that they never tried to do things any other way. Their way only works because that's their point of attraction.

Let me explain. Society says you must work hours for pay; you must give time for money to have a happy, successful life. So everyone follows the rules and works eight to ten hours per day for money. But what society fails to mention is the average nine-to-five worker is extremely unhappy, depressed, broke, and unfulfilled. Does society's way work? Yes, it does if you want those low vibrations. You can waste precious years, making pennies working for someone else's dream, or you can find your purpose right now. If you already know some of your life's purposes, then use this advice to enhance your goals.

Suppose you are already wealthy. You have plenty of savings, your family is well taken care of, and you have all your material desires (house, car, etc). Now suppose that no one in the world could judge you for what you wanted to do. What would you do every day without the worry or stress of life's materialistic world? Would you paint every day? Would you sing, act, or dance? Would you create a new way of using a cell phone? Would you take care of the elderly, and provide food for the homeless? Would you create a new board game? What about writing a book, or creating a script for a movie? What about inventing a new vegetable that kids will actually like? Would you talk to the urban youth? Would you create change for the upcoming generations? What would you really do without the pressure of society on your back? Whatever that is, that is your PURPOSE.

I'm not saying go quit your day job and draw pictures all day, but I am saying you should be making time to draw throughout the day if that is your passion. If you love drawing, you should be drawing in the morning, before bed, before watching TV, or even during your lunch break. You should learn how anime cartoon artists get reimbursed for drawing. Who pays artists? How can drawing a picture contribute to the world? Who are the highest-paid artists, and how did they turn their passion into money? Imagine growing up with no Disney movies because all of the artists who love to draw said, "I'll never make any money drawing. Let me just work at the factory with my dad. Let me be an adult and get a nine-to-five." What a sad childhood most of us would've had, never seeing color on the screen because it didn't fit into society's bubble.

We live in a time in which information is easily accessible. I mean, check out Google. You can find out how to do anything by modeling how others have done it before you. Of course, you should always add your own twist to ensure you are happy doing things your way. But the information is available. Other creative beings have made it easier for us. We can learn how to monetize our gifts. I'm not saying it will be easy, but neither is waking up every morning at six am to sit in traffic and work eight to ten hours for a paycheck that's owed to all of your creditors for the rest of your life. That doesn't seem very easy to me. If you have to choose between the two, why not take the path that leads to fulfillment?

Ok, let's say you figured out your purpose. Now how do you start living it? How do you get from under the shadow of what you are habitually used to doing on a daily basis? The answer is simple: just start. Mark Twain said, "The secret to getting ahead is to get started." I couldn't agree more. Start slow, start late, start hungry, start angry, but just start. Your natural intuition will kick in and start helping you get closer to your desires. This is a fact.

STORYTIME

"I hate that cubicle"

I learned my purpose many years ago when I discovered my love for books. As I briefly mentioned earlier, however, I didn't know how to become an author. Those short stories I wrote at the lunch table when I was in the first grade didn't quite convince me I had what it took. But writing always felt great, even then. My teachers were always impressed with how far I could go with my imagination, but like everyone else I was told to grow up, get a job, and blah blah blah. So like most of us, I never pursued my passions.

I started meditating and listening to positive content on YouTube. I became obsessed with learning the mind. The Law of Attraction made so much sense to me, and I started slowly putting it into practice. As my consciousness expanded, it became almost impossible to be mediocre. To do anything except my purpose was like fighting against myself. My higher self wanted me to cross over to the abundant life I deserved, but my lower self pleaded for my limitations. Society invented every possible reason why I should stay average.

My ego constantly tried to convince me that being an author was too hard, and I should just work a lousy job, pay my bills, and stay comfortable to ensure my security. As long as I made guaranteed bi-weekly money, which would always be there as long as I performed, I would be safe. My family and friends also agreed with my ego.

One random Wednesday morning, I sat in my little four-by-four cubicle in a black chair with two computer screens staring at me. I was a medical biller and coder. I spent most of my day begging insurance companies to pay their claims, speaking with angry patients and using online billing software. I spun in the office chair from boredom, until I became dizzy. I looked at the beautiful pictures of my children pinned to the thin cubicle walls. I peeked my head over at my coworker, who was typing one hundred words per minute. She looked overworked, stressed, and overwhelmed. I spun the chair again and glanced at the time on my computer, which read something like 11:37 am. Time was moving slowly.

I thought, "Damn, I really spend over eighty-five percent of my days in a freaking box!" I fell into a deep daydream as I looked at my surroundings. I stared at the pictures of my family, tacked to the flimsy fabric. Those pictures gave me hope on many days and also reminded me of my responsibilities as a single mother. I looked at the clock again, which now read 11:39 am. I had only wasted two lousy minutes.

I got up and walked to a coworker's desk to talk some trash, hoping to make the time go by faster. As I slowly walked back to my prison cell (my cubicle), I told myself, *If it's not lunchtime when I get back to my desk, I'm quitting.* I returned to my desk and the clock read, 11:51 a.m. At that moment I said to myself, *I never want to be in this box again.* I typed up my resignation letter and turned it in that day.

I quit so I could write my books and follow my purpose. I wanted to speak all over the world. I wanted to travel. I wanted to take care of my sick kids without receiving a write-up for calling out. I wanted to *live.*

My purpose called to me, and once I heard it clearly, nothing could stop me. I followed the *voice* and started creating my own reality.

Life Makes You Grow

LIFE HAS A WAY OF MAKING YOU MISERABLE IN ORDER TO HELP YOU GROW. It will not let you stay comfortable, and if you go against it, you will only become miserable. Life pulls you toward a higher you, and the more you resist it, the more you will feel uneasy, unworthy, or unfulfilled. Just like if you play a game on your phone, you have to level up. Once you beat that stage of the game, you are awarded a higher level, which is usually harder, but more fulfilling. Life is the exact same. You will keep losing until you win, but it will not let you go further until you level up.

Stop pulling back and go with it. If you don't know your purpose yet, life will show you. Deep down, I think most of us know, but we are scared to jump out there. Steve Harvey once said something that has always stayed with me. He said, "Jump and have faith the parachute will open." I've learned it will always open! Everything is always working out for us. It's our own limitations that slow down the manifestation process.

Following Your Purpose Requires Courage

EVERYONE CLOSE TO ME FLIPPED OUT WHEN I LEFT THE BOX! "How will you take care of your children?" they asked. I honestly didn't know the answer. I only knew at the time that I had a few thousand saved up. I had no plan, and my monthly expenses were over four thousand per month. My money would only last me three months, tops. I ignored the money and kept writing.

People told me writers don't really make money, and the chances of me living off a writer's salary were slim to none. I still kept writing. I used my other skills to make money, and money just came to me from everywhere. I can't even explain how I made it so long without a nine-to-five income. I started my own small business and I kept writing. Some of my investments failed. Some of my rent payments were late, but I still just kept writing.

I successfully published my first book, then my second. I then started making more money from motivational speaking, selling products, and trying different businesses. Most failed, but I just kept writing. I found myself being a serial entrepreneur. The ideas just kept coming and the money followed.

I wrote and produced a play called *DAMAGED*. I then published my third book, *Damien's Secret*, which resulted in me being introduced to the filming industry. I moved from Maryland to California and I just kept writing. Not once did I get evicted, get my car repossessed, or feel hunger pains from starvation. The universe worked it out. Money started working for me. Now by no means am I rich just yet, but I damn sure ain't broke, nor am I stuck in that box they call a cubicle.

I honestly didn't know how life would unfold, but I knew I had to keep writing. Because I didn't give up, you are now reading my eighth book. I even have three books in Spanish. Writing was the only thing that felt right. Whatever feels right to you, *that is your purpose*. It may be scary, but take the leap and I promise you won't regret your decision to do what you came to this planet to do.

The Three Roads In Life

I MADE THIS ANALOGY UP A FEW YEARS AGO TO REMIND MYSELF where I belong in life. It has helped me tremendously, and I hope it helps you, too. The basic idea is there are three roads in life. The road on the left is society's road. It has a guaranteed destination. The road on the right also has a destination, but it comes with a map. The road in the middle has no destination, nor does it come with any type of worldly guidance.

The road on the left

The road on the left, also known as society's road, tells you to work a full-time job, maybe have a kid, marry someone your family will love, keep your opinions to yourself, accept being average and unexceptional. Act like your culture and be just like your environment. Work until your life is over, and hope to live long enough to receive a retirement check so you can lie on a beach somewhere, old and wrinkled with your bones aching in the sand. But wait, the retirement check usually won't be enough to take care of you until you croak. So get a part-time job and continue to work until your death.

If you follow this road, you have a guarantee of normalcy. There is no risk on this road, no threats, and no need to ever be uncomfortable. A paycheck will come as long as you can physically chase it. Your path is clear. You came to the game of life to walk straight to your mediocre destination. Few will know you even ever existed, and many will choose to take the same road and be forgotten.

The road on the right

The road on the right is the middle-class road. Your destination is what is expected of you. You want a little more than what society says you can have. There are a few challenges on this road, but society gave you a map. It's the road of college, degrees, government jobs, middling cars, and decent houses. Because you want more on this road, you will have to push yourself. Sometimes the map is off and you will have to figure out things like how to pay for school, how to overcome poverty, and how to get a good spouse. This road is normal and not too exciting, but there are little fulfillments here and there. You sometimes feel like life is good. You still work, retire, and die. This road is a safe option, yet it comes with little adventure.

The road in the middle

The middle road is the road that you intended to take when you agreed to come to the game of life. You never wanted to be safe or have the road planned out for you. You intended to figure it out as you walked. There is no map! You don't know if you should go straight or turn, and that makes you uncomfortable—and you should be. When you get uncomfortable, you have to go to your inner being for guidance, and your spirit tells you which way to walk toward your destiny. Forget about the life society planned for you. The middle road is adventurous. It's filled with the unknown. Sometimes a tiger jumps out and scares the hell out of you, then you overcome the fear and become a lion. Sometimes you go the wrong way, which routes you on a new and unexpected journey that leads you closer to your destiny. Sometimes the road is filled with potholes, and you have to watch your steps to avoid falling. If you fall, you get back up and try again, making progress one step at a time.

On this middle road, you constantly have to think and listen for a higher power, because there is no map to guide you. You do things that bring you joy, you live life your way with no pre-planned direction, and you're able to just be. There are no time limits; you reach your destination whenever you get there. You make it to the beach before you are old and wrinkled. No pressure, no rules, no society, and no waiting for retirement. The middle road is for us people who came to play the game our way. Unfortunately, on this road you still will die—but oh, what a life you will be remembered for.

Find your purpose and choose your road. You can switch roads right now! You can live for *you* right now! The middle road is easy to get to from either side; just cross over. I'm waiting for you in the middle. Come find me in the next chapter. Flip the page when you're ready—I'm there waiting.

7

Craving Attention

"People with an unbridled thirst for attention is usually very empty and trying to fill themselves at the expense of others."

~ Amelia Rose

Why Do We Crave Attention?

LET'S BE HONEST. We all secretly want some kind of attention. It might be popularity, sexual interest, peer approval, or just likes on Instagram. But there's a huge problem with craving attention! The more we seek approval from others, the less we approve of ourselves. It's normal to want someone to compliment your nice outfit or your fresh haircut, but to seek the attention of other humans is a great disservice to your inner being.

There are five main reasons why we seek attention. Some of you might not like this, but hey, I had to face it too.

1. We are insecure

2. We are jealous

3. We never received attention

4. We lack confidence

5. We want to be seen

Attention & Insecurity

Insecure: *(of a person) not confident or assured; uncertain and anxious*

ALWAYS REMEMBER THIS: The loudest person in the room is the most insecure person in the room. They speak loudly to get the attention of everyone else. They demand to have the spotlight on them, even if the attention they receive is negative.

Some feel that being the center of attention makes them superior, and they feel they are conquering their insecurities because they are bold enough to overtalk everyone. Why should they feel bad about themselves for being bold? Rather than being embarrassed, they often feel we should admire their boldness because they have the balls to speak up.

Let's address this right now. If you are the loudest person in the room, be cool. Please don't be offended, if this is you. We do not judge in this book. Your insecurity is no worse than that of the quietest person in the room. This message is for everyone, whether you are too loud, too quiet, or in between. We all have insecurities. Address the things you don't like about yourself and learn to love them. Don't crave attention from other humans to validate the awesome person you are. Who are they? What significance do they really play in your reality?

So for my loud babies, chill out. We can hear you speaking. Would you speak that loud if you were talking to yourself? Probably not! So don't be loud to impress others or to be seen. Know who you are, and be comfortable in any situation just being you. For my quiet babies, speak up! So what if you think you sound stupid, or if others judge you because you're different? Who are they? Your voice matters, too. I've been both people. I've been drunk and loud. I've been scared and quiet. Neither person is me; it was all to fit in with the crowd. Now I just "BE."

Attention & Jealousy

Jealousy: *feeling or showing envy of someone or their achievements and advantages*

No one wants to be seen more than a jealous person. They want their ex's partner to see them. They want their old college competitors to see how well they are doing. They want the most popular girl from their childhood to admire them.

Jealous people tend to make up illusions in their minds about why someone has something they want, and they crave the attention of the very person they envy. I blame society for jealousy. They give us an image of what's perfect, and they drill it into our heads. Not just looks, but materialistic things as well. Society decided what was attractive and what was unattractive, and we found ourselves comparing and being jealous.

Here's what I want you to know so you will never feel envious again. The first thing to know is every human on this planet takes a dump. And it all stinks! They are no better than you. They have nothing you can't manifest yourself, as far as materialistic things go.

As far as looks are concerned, it's just a face. We all have one, and it holds no importance to eternity. I know in this material universe looks mean a lot to society, but it's only because society determined what beauty was and wasn't. If we judged each person strictly by their souls, oh what a beautiful place this would be.

When you get too caught up in your looks, ask yourself: *Am I going to choose Society or myself?* If you choose yourself, you instantly know that you are perfect. Your face doesn't make you smarter, it doesn't make your legs lift faster, it doesn't bring you closer to God, and it doesn't help you avoid cancer. As far as the universe is concerned, it holds no value. You are beautiful and there will never be another you. Don't waste another minute comparing or envying another human. You are too special to waste energy on what others appear to have.

Think of this the next time you crave attention. The sun comes out every day to provide light, heat, and food, yet it never asks for your praise. The sun never craves attention from humans for all it does for us, nor does it envy the moon. It's confident in knowing it's the sun; it requires no validation. Be humble and confident that nothing around you matters as much as you matter to yourself. Jealousy is for the weak, and no one holding or listening to this book is weak.

Attention & the Lack Of It

Lack: *the state of being without or not having enough of something*

IF A PERSON NEVER RECEIVES ATTENTION, THEY TEND TO GROW UP LOOKING FOR IT. Maybe they were constantly ignored and now they crave for their voice to be heard. This type of attention seeker is stuck telling an old story.

Feel your left pinky right now. Rub it from the nail bed to the knuckle. Look at all the lines on your pinky. Can you feel me touching your pinky? Am I important in your intimate moment with you rubbing your pinky? Are you thinking of how I'm ignoring you while you touch your pinky? No! That is your pinky, and you feel *your* own sense of touch, and you are looking at the lines on *your* hands from *your* own eyes. You don't need anyone's attention to exist in this life. You got this, all by yourself. If people ignored you a lot, good! It gave you time to listen to yourself.

Attention & Confidence

Confidence: *a feeling of self-assurance arising from one's appreciation of one's own abilities or qualities*

WHEN YOU ARE CONFIDENT, PEOPLE SEE IT IN THE WAY YOU WALK. You never need society's approval. You know who you are. When you lack confidence, you starve for attention because you are searching for people to validate who you are. You want them to make you feel more secure. You feed off their energy and you impatiently wait for all eyes to be on you.

A person with confidence never searches the room for eye contact. They know who they are no matter who is in the room. So how do you gain confidence? Just be bold with your choices and don't consider anyone else when making them.

For example: Wear what you want and don't worry that maybe it's too flashy, too boring, too colorful, or too sexy. Pick out what you want, wear it, and feel good in it. Suppose you reach your destination and everyone is wearing dresses and suits, but you chose a blouse and jeans. Boy, are you lucky! You get to be comfortable, you get to dance freely while everyone else's feet hurt from fancy shoes, you get to stand out without searching for attention. You will be remembered, and you will go home feeling true to your comfortable self. Never lack confidence, and be true to yourself. After all, you are stuck with yourself for eternity, not with someone else.

Confidence is so important as we live this experience. There is actually a law in the universe called "the Law of Confidence." To be confident is to be beyond any limitations anyone else can put on you. It takes great confidence to believe in yourself. Anything you want to manifest must first start with a belief that you can have it. Then you must have the confidence to go and get it.

Confidence starts with knowing who you are and being extremely comfortable in your own skin. Start looking in the mirror and really see yourself. Look deep in your eyes and search for the *you* beyond the skin. Tell yourself, *I matter. I'm just as important as anyone else. No one has anything that I don't. This is my journey and I'm the best player for this life. I'm on this planet so I can have anything. I'm worthy of everything. I'm me. I love me.*

I once heard the body referred to as "the meat suit." That cracked me up. That's exactly what it is. Our spirit borrows this meat suit to experience life with our senses in order to interpret this reality. We started as swimming sperm with no limbs. Our energy/spirit jumped into the sperm, and the process started to create the perfect meat suit for us. We began growing bones, legs, arms, toes, eyes, etc. You were specially made by a higher power. You have to look beyond the meat suit, because it's the spirit that jumped into the body that deserves all your attention.

We care so much about our physical appearance, even though we know we won't be physical beings forever. We won't be this young forever, we won't have this same exact body build forever, we won't even have this body forever. Be confident in knowing nothing can break your spirit. It's eternal. It outlives all embarrassment, all heartbreaks, all insecurities, all shame, and all doubt. It outlives all made-up problems. Insert confidence into your spirit. Know who you are. Know what you can do. Know no one can stop you.

***

STORYTIME

"Janice"

There was a girl whom I'll never forget who went to my high school. Let's just call her Janice. She was constantly teased and bullied. She wasn't in any of my classes, but I would see her around the hallways and at lunch.

One day Janice was walking down the hallway when two boys kicked her in the back of her knees and she fell right on her face. Her books flew up in the air, and I remember she just lay there. She didn't jump right up. Many people laughed, especially the girls. Some screamed, "Get up dumb-dumb!" She just sat there with her face planted on the cold floor.

I walked over to her, with everyone watching, and reached my hand out. She screamed, "Just leave me alone!" Now the crowd was yelling remarks to me: "Sunni, you need to mind your own business. Ms. Ugly doesn't even want your help." I ignored them and reached out my hand again. She didn't grab it, but this time she didn't yell either. The bell rang and everyone stepped over her as they made their way to their next class. Once the hallway was almost clear, she grabbed my hand, which was still extended, and stood up. It was the most exhilarating feeling to have her accept my help.

"I hate this school," she said as she started picking up her books.

I helped her gather her papers and replied, "What's your name?"

"Janice. You're Sunni, right?"

"Yup. Do you live around here?" I asked as I fetched another one of her books.

"I live with my father on Harford Road. My mother died when I was four," she softly replied.

"Dag, I'm sorry. I couldn't imagine. So, it's just you and your dad?"

"And my little brother. He doesn't look like me, though. He looks more like my mom. She was pretty like you, but I look like my father." She lowered her head.

I paused, not knowing what to say next. "Thanks, but you look exactly how you should look. I think you are kind of cool." I smiled.

"I look in the mirror and I hate what I see, but I look just like my father and he's my best friend. He's the best father in the world, and he loves me and my brother so much." A tear rolled down her eye.

"Do you think your father is ugly?" I asked with sympathy.

"No. He never looks ugly to me."

"So who cares what everyone says? You look like your best friend. Your father seems cool! I'm a daddy's girl, too. Now stop crying because I don't hang out with cry babies." I laughed. "Come on, let's skip class."

"Girl, I don't skip class. I'm on the honor roll," she said seriously.

We both burst out laughing. "Well, Ms. Honor Roll, you are already late. People are just waiting to talk crap about you when you get in the class, anyway. The next time you fall, get up quick. Never let them see you sweat."

I pulled her arm and she hesitantly went with me. We talked about her entire life, and I soon discovered she was one of the most beautiful people I had ever met. Her spirit was filled with love and positive energy. She was excited to be with someone who treated her with respect, and I was excited to be around someone whose heart was so pure. From that day forward, if I saw her, I would walk past her lunch table and say, "Hey, Ms. Honor Roll." She always smiled and shied away.

As the school year went on, she gained a few friends and her confidence went through the roof. She started walking tall, and as soon as someone talked crap about her, she was ready to say something back. I was so proud.

I tell this story because Janice found something inside herself. If nothing else, she felt proud to look like someone she loved so much. Once she became comfortable with who she was, her confidence gave her power, and no one could break her after she gained self-esteem. Her appearance was really no one's business, and the same people who teased her were the same attention seekers who were insecure about themselves. What Janice didn't know was that I had my own insecurities.

Just a few weeks before I met Janice, a boy in my class tried to break my confidence. He had chunky thighs, a weird complexion, and a slight lisp when he talked. He said something to me that I will never forget.

We had a substitute teacher, and we all sat around talking and doing nothing. I sat at a table with two other girls and about five boys. One of the boys asked

Chunky Thighs, "Who would you make your girl-friend out of everyone in the class?"

He answered, "Renee, but I would choose Sunni if she dressed better. She's pretty and I like her personality, but she doesn't have any clothes."

OUCH! That really stung, and he said it right in front of everyone, including me. I felt so low and just wanted to hide in a corner. I thought, *Calm down, Chunky Thighs. You couldn't get me to be your girl if all I wore was a pillowcase.* That's what I thought, but I didn't say anything to defend myself. I just stayed quiet. A few girls laughed, and my self-esteem dropped by the minute.

Here I was, thinking no one really noticed my lack of clothes, which was due to poverty and life circum-stances. I was always clean—I just didn't have money, so I sometimes wore the same jeans from the prior week. I never really thought anyone paid that much attention. I never got bullied or teased for not having as many clothes as some of the other kids had.

Although the guy wasn't my type and I shouldn't have cared if he liked me or not, I still felt the need to justify myself to Mr. Chunky Thighs. My goal became to get clothes, by any means necessary. I deserved to look nice, like all the other girls in high school. I won't get too deep into the things I started doing to make money – you can get that tea from my memoirs – but let's just say that by the time I entered the eleventh grade, I had a lot of clothes.

I wasn't craving attention, but I did lack confidence. The two go hand in hand. Because I lacked confidence, the fresher my clothes got, the more I wanted to be seen. I yearned for validation. I got a high if someone complimented what I wore, and I started expecting that type of attention.

One day I was getting dressed in front of the mirror, and I was thinking about what I had done to get the clothes. I looked in the mirror completely naked and asked myself, "Now with no clothes on, who are you? What changed?" The answer was nothing. I looked at my hand like I had when I was young, and I remembered that I was a soul. From that day forward, I stopped trying to impress others with clothes and I started impressing myself.

Now let's be real. I still wanted to look nice. I never wanted to be the girl with no clothes again, and I was too immature to comprehend that people's opinions didn't determine who I was. I now know that while I'm on this unlimited place called a planet, I can have whatever I want, and clothes are such a small thing compared to all that's here. Of course, I'm worthy enough to have clothes.

Because this is my book and I can do whatever I want (*See my confidence there?*), I would like to take a moment to thank Mr. Chunky Thighs for allowing me to learn the self-esteem lesson early in life. I also want to thank Janice for teaching me beauty is within. As I play the game of life, I'm grateful for every experience, including this one. I still love the right kind of attention, but I'll never crave it. You should never crave attention! There is an entire universe that gives you undivided attention and focuses on your very existence. People's opinions are small compared to all that you are. You are much more than I can even explain. Tap into that power, and be confident in every situation.

8

Protect Your Energy

"It is your divine right and your spiritual duty to protect your energy field from unwanted influences. In the wise words of the Mahatma, do not allow anyone to walk through your mind with their dirty feet."

~ Anthon St. Maarten

What Is That?

Boom, boom, boom. My heart is racing. I feel uncomfortable inside. It's an uneasy feeling in my chest. It's not butterflies, it's not quite fear, so what is it? Oh, It's bad energy. I can't think of anything more important for your well-being than your energy. Now, if I'm being honest, I must admit that protecting my energy is something I have really struggled with over the years. I feel it would be unfair to give advice about something I haven't personally experienced. In this chapter, we will speak of energy in the emotional sense, not in the scientific sense. There's a section dedicated to parents, but even if you are not a parent, you are someone's child. I believe it will be beneficial for everyone to read this entire chapter.

What Is Emotional Energy?

Emotional energy is the energy behind your emotions. This could be emotions you caused yourself, or emotions you allowed yourself to feel from others.

What Affects Your Emotional Energy?

I HATE TO SAY THIS, but it's often the people you love the most and the people you are around the most who affect your emotional energy.

How Do You Control Your Emotions When Your Energy Is Impacted?

FIRST, CHOOSE YOURSELF. That is the hardest thing to do when you love others. Trust me, I know. You must find a way to get back to your well-being when your emotions are out of control. If you take everyone else out of the equation, you realize you actually feel okay on the inside. The problem is, we are not on this planet alone, so others can block our energy, but only if we let them.

Society's Version Of A Parent

DID YOU KNOW THE AVERAGE PARENT IS MISER-ABLE? No one ever discusses the stress, torture, and emotional imbalance one must endure to be called "Mommy" or "Daddy." Society is lying once again. They put the parent role on such a high pedestal, and we try to live up to what a mother or father should be. The truth is, though, we are just trying to figure out our own place in life. How dare society put pressure on us as parents to make perfect human beings who stay out of trouble and make the choices we believe they should make? Who said that was our job? And who made the job so hard? We are all someone's child. And we all grew up and went on our own journey. Why is the pressure on the parent/creator?

Society got it fucked up. They enslave parents to their children. We cater to them instead of loving them. We should be guiding them as best as possible and letting them become. We don't own our children. They are God's children. They are a part of this universe like everyone else. Trying to control them stops their creativity.

Serving them causes us as parents a great deal of stress. Society tells us that we must feed them first, do everything for them, take on all their emotions, and accept the blame if they come out screwed up in any way. Children are demanding energy suckers, and if you are not careful you will be miserable in your own home. Yup, I said it! I did the unthinkable. I exposed the truth. It's time we stop faking and start living.

Do kids bring us joy? Absolutely! They are awesome! They can turn a bad day into a good one. Can they also bring us pain? Absolutely! They can turn a good day into a bad one. That problem is not our children's fault; they are just being them. The problem is our fault because we are not controlling our emotions. No one should have the power to change our day from good to bad. Only we can do that, because it's our day! We have to learn to choose the battles we are willing to give our energy to. We cannot give our energy to every situation. I struggled with this quite a bit. I cared too much! Although I cared a lot, I still would choose my energy over someone else's when I was conscious enough to realize what was happening.

I couldn't understand how I allowed my children to get me so upset. Even with all this information I knew about the mind, I allowed my mind to be compromised by my children. They had the power to change my day in a matter of seconds. I instantly felt every emotion they felt. If one of my kids was upset or crying, I would become upset before I even knew what was wrong. Their emotions immediately jumped into my energy. I constantly reacted without protecting my energy.

Sometimes as a mother, I found myself feeling low for some of the choices I made while parenting. There is no such thing as a perfect parent, nor is there such a thing as a perfect child. With those two facts alone, you would think we would take it a little easier on ourselves. Parenting doesn't come with a rulebook, and if you are following society's standards they will tell you that we parents screw up quite a bit. But if you are following real-life standards, we are all doing the best we are capable of doing at that precise moment.

While I was struggling with my flaws as a parent, my soulmate gave me some great advice that stuck with me, and I would like to share it with you.

"Calmly get to the root of the problem and ignore all the little details."

That statement can be used in any kind of problem-solving situation, not only for parents. Imagine a tree with roots sinking deep into the soil. For that tree to grow, you must take care of the roots. The leaves on the tree represent all the little details. Yes, they are important but they are not what makes the tree grow. It's usually the details that get us so upset. If you calmly deal with the root of the problem, it can be handled more efficiently. The details are usually over-exaggerated and made out to be more dramatic than needed. It's a way for someone else to immediately get you on their side or make the issue seem worse than it is. Don't focus on the details, just simply ask yourself what the real problem is. Remember: Your mind makes up problems, too, so make sure the issue is really something that requires a solution. If not, let the other person figure it out on their own.

We Mattered Before We Became Parents

WE ARE INDIVIDUALS FIRST AND PARENTS AFTER. Society can't tell us what a perfect parent is, how we should act toward our children, or whether we should take every emotion they feel and make it ours. Of course, we will have moments when we hurt because our kids hurt. But choose when you hurt. If your child is upset because they can't go outside, that shouldn't make you upset. If your child is suffering from their first heartbreak, that may hurt you, so hug them and feel what they feel. But you cannot feel all their emotions. If they have an attitude, so be it. Go take a walk and leave them right there with their attitude.

This may feel like a touchy subject for some parents. Some may even feel guilty or offended. I completely understand. When I first became a parent I gave my entire life to the new duties of trying to make my little babies something in this world. I forgot about myself and the things I'd enjoyed before giving birth. That went on for years. I was no longer Sunni; I became a mother and that was it. My entire existence was on the back burner for ten years. When I realized I had become invisible in my own reality, I made it my purpose to find myself again. I started doing things for myself and finding "me time" throughout the day. It was amazing getting to know myself again. It was a struggle for the kids, because they felt like I belonged to them and I should be serving them at all times. It's okay, because sometimes kids get confused about life, and them thinking they own you is proof they can get extremely confused.

Just know it's okay to feel overwhelmed, used, unappreciated, and tired as a parent. Don't feel guilty for sometimes wanting to escape from them little buggers. They didn't bring you into their reality—you brought them into yours. You were a carrier to provide them with life, and they don't run you. You are not here to serve children. Do some things for yourself, incorporate them into your reality, and ignore what society has to say about it, because those same kids will grow up and do their own thing. You don't own them; they are free spirits and one day they will be making their own choices. Learn to balance your personal identity with your parental identity.

STORYTIME

"Don't answer the phone"

One day I was feeling great. I rode on the highway with the windows down, the breeze blowing through my hair. I was daydreaming about all the positive things I wanted to accomplish. I drove in silence, not even bothering to cut on the radio. I was mesmerized by the beautiful sky, and I was silently speaking gratitude for being alive.

My peaceful moment was interrupted by a phone call. I looked at the phone and considered ignoring it. I wanted to continue floating down the highway in my zone. The person called three more times and, regrettably, I answered the phone. On the other end of the phone line awaited drama. "Hello," I calmly answered, still floating in my zone.

With irritation, the person screeched, "Damn, I've been calling you all day. Why didn't you answer? I had a horrible fucking day. First let me tell you what happened at work."

I held the phone and thought to myself, *She didn't even ask how I was doing or anything*. That person just wanted to release their negative energy onto someone, and I was the dummy that answered the phone. The aggressive tone of her voice gave me anxiety, and I instantly allowed her anger into my energy. I decided not to speak much and just let her vent. The entire conversation was about everything that was going wrong in her life. She didn't have one positive thing to say. By the time we hung up the phone, I was upset and my vibration was low.

It took me quite some time to bring myself back to a normal state. I couldn't get back to the vibe I'd had before answering the phone. The good-feeling ride was now overwhelming and heavy. As I gazed at the sky, I finally heard *the voice*. My inner being informed me that that person's problem was not my problem, and those were not my emotions. I now know that to protect my energy I must get back to daydreaming. I also know I don't have to answer the phone the next time, because protecting my energy is more important than being a listening ear for someone's drama.

Choose When To Deal With Others' Energy

PEOPLE CAN BE EXTREMELY DRAINING. Have you noticed? They feel they can just load you with a bunch of their heavy mess, and like a fool we gladly accept their junk. There's a huge difference between being a supportive friend and being a crutch for someone's emotions. Stay away from all the negative Nancys—they are the worst type of energy suckers. Unfortunately, you can't avoid people altogether, but you can learn to choose when to deal with their energy.

The signs of an energy sucker are usually pretty clear early on. Don't ignore those signs. Most of the time it can be the very first sentence of a conversation, whether it be on a phone call or in person. That first sentence tells you everything. Listen to their tone, the volume of their voice, and their anxiousness to talk first. Once you recognize the signs, it's up to you to continue with the conversation. You could pretend someone is on the other line and ditch the call. You could excuse yourself and walk away. I'm usually the honest type. If you really want to be honest, you can politely say, "Girl, I love you but this is too heavy for me today."

You may want to be that supportive person, and sometimes you're in the right space to help someone who is having a bad day. That's fine as well. Just make sure you are in the right space. Don't be floating down the highway and take on their energy. That would be taking your time away from God. Great thoughts come to you when you are in that peaceful space. Don't lose those precious moments for an unworthy negative experience.

Strangers can affect your energy, too!

One night I was on my way home. I stopped at a gas station to get some gas and a bottle of water, that's all. I walked in behind a young lady who let the door go instead of holding it for me. I thought to myself, *That was rude.* I walked into the chaotic environment. The energy in the gas station was horrible. A lady was arguing with the counter clerk, people in line were complaining about how long they had been waiting, and children were running around. One of the kids bumped into me, and I accidentally dropped everything out of my purse.

I walked right into an energy-sucking environment. Instead of getting upset, I laughed and picked up all my items from the floor. I calmly put everything back into my purse. I returned the water bottle to the refrigeration section and kindly walked my happy ass back to my car. There was another gas station right across the street. I drove over, walked in, and was greeted by the friendly clerk. There was only one person in line and the transaction was smooth. This is a prime example of how you can easily protect your energy from strangers.

Sometimes you can walk into a space and feel bad energy. If I'm able to walk back out, that's what I do. However, there are those moments when you are in the supermarket with all your groceries on the belt and the cashier is being downright rude. You likely don't want to pack all that food back into the cart, so what do you do? I first try to remind myself that the person is a stranger who means nothing to me because

I don't know them. Unfortunately, sometimes my ego takes over and wants to jump across the counter and scratch the person's eyeballs out. I never do, though, but instead, I talk myself into allowing everyone to feel how they feel.

I never know what could've happened to make that person behave that way. They could be bitter for many reasons. It would be insane for me to jump on their bitter bandwagon and become catty with them. That would mean lowering my vibration down to a stranger's vibration without even knowing what their issue is. It's not worth it. Just smile and leave that bitterness with the original owner.

Decide What Kind Of Friend You Want To Be

BEING A FRIEND CAN BE A CHALLENGING TASK. You must decide what kind of friend you want to be. Are you the drama friend? Are you the gossiping friend that feeds off the latest news? Are you an uplifting friend, who encourages and mostly calls with good news? Are you a draining friend, who always calls with some sad story? Are you the friend who only calls when you need something? You can be whatever kind of friend you want, but just know you play a role in the energy you give off. We don't just accept others' energies—we release energy as well.

I'm now the friend you don't call with nonsense because my energy shows I don't want to hear it. I'm not going to entertain the gossip, and people can feel it. Don't get me wrong, though: I'll listen to a little tea. But I have things to do, so usually, I don't have much time for that. Now, if you call me about a new business idea or how you are growing in your life, then I will be ecstatic. I've lost many friends because I chose to protect my energy. I no longer have anything in common with them. They feel I've changed, I feel I've grown. We don't have the same energy anymore. We don't do the same things anymore, and that's okay. One thing we must never do is try to keep people in our lives longer than a season. We get a lot of seasons in the game, and more are guaranteed to come. If those friends' seasons are over, it's okay to let them go.

One mistake we often make is holding onto time. Time is not to be held; we live in a timeless universe. We will literally make ourselves miserable because of the time we've invested in a relationship. I've witnessed horrible friendships with bad energy and I've asked, "Why are guys even friends?" The response is almost always the same. "I've known her or him since I was a kid." So, because you knew someone since you were a kid, you have to keep them in your life forever?

Everything changes in life, and when your friends are no longer on your vibration, it's time for new friends. Their season is over. This may seem harsh, but you cannot effectively grow while doing the same things and hanging with the same people. Life is about expansion. You should always want more, and you must surround yourself with others who want more. Don't feel guilty for outgrowing certain people in your life. It's okay. We are only here on earth for a short time, and you don't have to spend all your time with the same people, in the same neighborhood, who are doing the same things. Get new friends who are doing new things. Don't put too much pressure on the word "loyalty." You must be loyal to yourself first.

Lastly, find friends with good energy. Find friends who are excited about your good news. Find friends who can educate you. Find friends who are willing to teach you how they received their abundance. Find friends who laugh and make you feel good. Find friends that share your vibration. They are out there. You attract who you are. If you can't understand why your growth is stagnant, just take a look around and see who you are hanging out with, and that should answer your question.

It Takes Work To Protect Your Energy

I WANT YOU TO LEARN THE BRUSH-OFF METHOD. When an energy sucker comes around and gets you upset, I want you to take your hand and brush their energy off your heart. You have to physically do it. Then ask yourself, "What do I feel right now? Is it my energy or theirs?" Then brush your heart again while taking a deep breath. At that moment, you get to choose. At first, your emotions chose for you by just accepting the energy in the room, but once you acknowledge that it's not YOUR energy, you then have the power!

Understand this: We are all a work in progress. You can't just read a book and say, "Fuck society," and live happily ever after. Every day you must work on yourself to be the best person you possibly can be in each moment. You notice I said, "each moment." That's all we have. We only have the moment we are in right now. Remember: We always move forward on the game board. Whatever way you reacted is how you felt at that moment, and so what? Try to do better next time. It's never wrong because an experience can't be wrong. They are your emotions, and you reacted based on how you felt. But if you truly want to be happy, you have to control your emotions and protect your energy.

Walk Away

IT'S OKAY TO WALK AWAY FROM YOUR FAMILY and let them figure it out on their own. It's okay to ignore a friend's call and let them complain to someone else. It's okay to leave a store filled with drama to protect your peace. Here's something I really want you to know: You come first at all times. This may seem selfish, but who are you with 24/7? Yourself! Right? You always have to choose yourself first, or you won't be any good for anyone else.

I sometimes still struggle to control my emotions. If someone close to me is upset, I may get upset because I want to help them feel better. I want to provide a solution or some advice on how to confront the issue. But the truth is, they will just have to figure it out by themselves (which they probably prefer anyway). As much as I would love to help, I have to let them figure it out to protect my energy. So I walk away and give that person space. Being who you truly are requires you to walk away quite a bit.

If someone is yelling, walk away. If someone is trying to push their beliefs on you, walk away. If someone is constantly complaining, walk away. If someone is gossiping, walk away. You always have a choice, and the choice must always be to put yourself first. Protect your MF energy at all costs, and don't let anyone disrupt your peace. Don't feel guilty—feel proud, and continue letting the wind blow in your hair.

Why Was This Book Released Over Three Years Late?

THIS BOOK WAS ORIGINALLY WRITTEN IN 2019, but because I hadn't actually learned how to protect my energy, I refused to release the book. How could I advise people how to live better when I hadn't figured it out for myself? I knew all the rules, but I still couldn't control my emotions. I couldn't understand why I didn't apply the tools to my own life. I wrote them, so why was I still an emotional wreck? Why was I still letting people piss me off and suck up my energy? Why was I allowing people to turn my good day into a bad one?

If I was really creating my own reality, and if I really had the control to make my life better, then why was I still getting stuck with this energy part of the game? It's simple: because I wasn't putting myself first. Once I figured that out, I was comfortable sharing these tools because I knew they worked. Actually applying the changes is the real challenge. That's why this is not a book you give away; this is a book you keep so you can revisit it. That's what I did. I constantly picked up the little black and white book (that's what I call it) and read my own advice and applied it for that day. I literally went to whatever chapter I needed and applied the prescribed action.

Now, why am I telling you this? These are details you never had to know. I'm telling you this because in order for your life to work, you have to do the work. For you to choose your higher self over the version society has enforced you to be, you have to believe in yourself. You are the answer. Everything you need to protect your energy is inside you, not in people or circumstances. That sounds easy, but you must practice with yourself. Ask yourself, "How does this make me feel?" and if it doesn't feel good, you need to choose another option. Protecting your energy is your biggest task in life. It's what keeps that smile on your face. Circumstances and challenges will always come up, but how you handle them is what determines the kind of life you will live. Play the game to win!

9

Money Does Grow On Trees

"Success is my idol and being broke is my rival."

~ Big Sean

Trees = Paper

Paper = A Bunch Of Money

TREES GROW PAPER EVERY DAY, and money is made out of paper. I say we need to start hugging more trees.

Society told me that I was destined for poverty; that people like me don't make millions, and people who grew up in my neighborhood won't have a shot at a successful life; that my environment was as far as I would go with a limited mind. I can't tell you how many times I heard, "Money doesn't grow on trees." Adults would say things like, "We can't afford that," or "That's too expensive." It took me years to get these poor thought patterns out of my memory.

Do you think one could ever count all the trees in the universe? There are trees in abundance! You can have whatever you want. If it's here, you can have it. Who are people to make you think life is limited? Why not tell a child they can have their biggest desires? Why set them up to think so little when life shows you everything so big? Is the sky little? Are there only a small number of trees? Is the ocean so small that we can barely see it? What about the sun? Do we need a microscope to see it? Are there only five cars in the universe, or are there highways filled with cars? Nothing on this entire planet is lacking, and that includes money! If you believe money is hard to obtain, then it will be. If you believe you can have as much money as you want while you have breath in your body, you can. So let's discuss this big topic that scares ninety-five percent of the population.

What Is Money?

- Paper

- Energy

- Luxury

MONEY IS A PIECE OF *PAPER* that you accumulate based on your *energy, and* it allows you the *luxury* to get the things you want. Nothing more, nothing less. There are many ways to attract money. It's funny that society only talks about one method. That method is labor for money, also known as time for money. This chapter is not to convince you to quit your nine-to-five job. This chapter is to open your mind about your perceptions of money. I had a huge fear of money. I felt like it was hard to get, hard to keep, and hard to grow. Soon as I got it, I had to pay bills, save some of it, or buy a few things I wanted. My relationship with money was awful. I felt abandoned because it always left me.

Here's my new understanding of money. We live in a vibrational universe, and where we place our attention and energy is important because it determines what we will attract. To say it simply: We must stop putting money on a pedestal as if it's different from anything else we want to obtain.

Treat money like you would a t-shirt. Does it seem impossible to own twenty t-shirts? Do you think in a lifetime you could manifest these shirts? I think you could. Money works the same way. You can manifest how much you want based on how much you **believe** you can actually obtain. The first thing that must be done is to change your beliefs about money. All those cliche lessons you heard growing up need to be removed from your mind right now and thrown away. No more poverty talk. The first time you hear yourself thinking in a lackful way, address it. Remind yourself you are unlimited, and that negative thought isn't true.

You can afford anything here on this planet. If it exists, you can have it. That may seem unrealistic based on your beliefs, and I understand why. Trust me, I've been there. A belief is something you think is true based on evidence. So, because you've been poor more than you've been rich, it feels true to believe it's hard to get money or to keep money. But if your belief was based on what's possible, then you could easily open the doors of abundance.

Just because you believe something doesn't mean it's true. It just means it's something you experienced in the past, so your mind has made it true. You have to take your power back from money! It doesn't own you. Instead of working for it, make *it* work for you.

As a kid, my beliefs about money sucked. My environment tried to mold me into a poverty magnet. I constantly questioned why I couldn't have everything I wanted. It was right there in the store, so why did I never have enough? I was grateful for what I had, but I was never satisfied.

—ell—

STORYTIME

"THE DAY I BECAME "Mentally Rich"

When I was a little girl, I remember going into the corner store with a friend. I had fifty cents and she had one dollar. She bragged the entire walk to Mr. Lee's store, saying how she had a whole dollar and she was going to buy this and that. Usually, most things in the corner store were only twenty-five cents, like the can sodas, ice cream sandwiches, bags of chips, and so on. Well, this day, we discovered Mr. Lee's prices had gone up, and now chips were thirty-five cents a bag, which left me without enough to get two items as I had planned.

"Mr. Lee, why are the chips thirty-five cents now?" I quickly asked.

Yelling from behind the counter, he said, "That's the new price, that's the new price."

"Why? They were always twenty-five cents."

"You girls buy something or go!" Mr. Lee demanded.

"Come on, let's go to the other store." I grabbed my friend's arm.

"Look at the bag," he quickly said, realizing we were about to go somewhere else. "That is the new price. It's on the bag. New store, same price."

I grabbed the bag of chips and discovered that thirty-five cents was indeed the price printed on the bag. My heart was crushed. Growing up, we depended on things being twenty-five cents, especially chips. That always meant a dollar could get you four items. I now didn't have enough for chips and a drink. I grabbed the bag of chips and got three five-cent Laffy Taffys and left the store disappointed.

This is how poor my mindset was. An increase in pricing made my little eight-year-old heart ache. This is not the day I became mentally rich, if you were wondering. This is the day I felt lackful. This story will probably make my mother cringe because she always made sure we had enough. When you are poor, enough is all you get. I could've run home and gotten a dime from my mother, but that didn't cross my mind. The only thing that crossed my mind was that I didn't have enough.

A child growing up in Beverly Hills would never discuss how much a bag of chips cost. Something as petty as chips are so small compared to the amount of abundance they've been shown. Their parents don't create a narrative of poverty in their experience, so they are not even aware that a bag of chips could be expensive for some people. But I was aware, and that kind of lackful talk became part of my makeup.

It wasn't until I was an adult that I started to change that lackful talk, but it wasn't easy. I read many books on the topic of money. They talked about the mind and money, manifesting money, investing money, and saving money. If you name it, I read it. As I read, I took little principles from each book. But it wasn't until later that I realized money wasn't the issue. There's plenty of money on this planet. The US prints about 38 million notes a day, which comes to about $541 million. That's per day! It is said that ninety-five percent of the money is used to replace old notes. So clearly there's enough money for more of us to be abundant.

If the issue wasn't lack of money, because there is more than enough on the planet, then I realized the issue had to be lack itself. Having a lackful mindset is what stops abundance from entering your experience. It was lackful thinking that kept me broke. It was having the mindset that there was never enough; doing things like counting my items before I reached the register to make sure I had enough, and checking the price of every single item. It was all that penny-pinching that kept me broke.

The day I became mentally rich was the day I stopped feeling lackful, knew I had enough, and stopped caring about prices and just threw the items in the cart. You have to become mentally rich before you will ever see any wealth on the outside. What you believe is a mirror of your reality. Most lottery winners go broke because although they have the physical money, they are still poor on the inside. I changed my mindset to abundance. I constantly reminded myself there was so much here, and I was worthy of abundance. I looked to nature to confirm that there is no lack on this planet, so why would ninety-five percent of humans live in lack? The answer was simply that ninety-five percent of people believe there's not enough. The other five percent are wealthy, and they believe in the opposite of lack.

Two Valid Reasons To Spend Money

#1. Purchasing something to make you better

<u>Here are a few examples</u>

- Healthy food

- Workout equipment

- Self-help book

- Meditation Retreat/Motivation seminar

- Online course

- Vitamins, herbs, etc.

It's pretty much anything that enhances you as a person: enhances your body, so you can live longer; enhances your mind so you can feel better; and enhances your soul so you can get closer to the real you.

#2. Investing in something to make you more money

<u>Here are a few examples</u>

- Product for your new business

- Business seminar

- Hiring an expert in your field

- Furniture for your new office

- Assets

- Supplies, promotional materials, etc.

- Investments, stocks, retirement, etc.

This second way of spending money enhances your business (if you have one) so you can make more money, enhances your business relationships so you can learn from others, and enhances your knowledge so you can continue to make money in your field. If you don't have a business, the same rule applies: You should be investing money every time you get paid. Of course, you want to enjoy your money as well, but just know in those moments of blowing money, you are not making it and you are not investing it. So, until you are comfortable with your finances, you should try to limit your spending.

What Separates The Poor From The Rich?

IF WE ALL HAVE THE SAME ORGANS, brains, and body functions as any other human, then we can do the same things they do to create generational wealth. In my opinion, there are only three things that separate the poor from the rich.

1. Knowledge/ information

2. Mindset

3. Relationships

#1 Knowledge / Information

KNOWLEDGE IS A MUST IN ORDER TO BE PART OF THE FIVE PERCENT. You must feed your mind with information daily, because if you don't, your mind will hold onto old data that you were already taught. You don't need to know how to make forty thousand dollars a year—you already know that (that's old data). You need to know how to make a few million dollars a year. Only learning new information can tell you how to achieve things you never had. You have to study what millionaires do. How do they move? What are their conversations like?

I once sat at a table with a few millionaires and a few thousandaires and I noticed something profound. The millionaires didn't gossip or talk about senseless things. They talked obsessively about what they wanted to do next. One of the young ladies spoke about how owning a basketball team was on her bucket list. She spoke highly and confidently about how she would bring the first NBA team to Baltimore. No one questioned whether that was possible. No one gave every reason in the book why it wouldn't work, or told her it was an admirable dream but no way would a black woman ever own a basketball team. Instead, they all encouraged her idea because they had millionaire mindsets.

Some of us at the table weren't quite there yet financially, but we had the right mindset. We had a high enough frequency to be at that table. You must learn to be who you want to be, and that doesn't involve trying to emulate someone else. You must study the information and put yourself around people who have the knowledge to help you level up.

Your broke-ass friends can't tell you anything about a level they've never been on. It's like someone who's never even been on an elevator trying to explain the penthouse. You can't ask them, "How is it at the top?" because they don't know. They haven't experienced it. However, you can read a book explaining not only how to build the elevator to take you to the penthouse, but also how to design a penthouse. You can learn how to make enough money so that every time you travel you can stay in a penthouse. Or you can sit at a table with people who can tell you all about how it is at the top. Either way, it's knowledge or information. Don't try to get that information from people who have never been on that high level. They are incapable of helping you do something, since they've never done it.

#2 Mindset

THE SECOND THING THAT SEPARATES THE POOR FROM THE RICH IS MINDSET. To truly build a wealthy mindset involves more than just using wishful affirmations. We are in a vibrational universe that requires action. We can't just sit around and do affirmations all day. We must apply action as well. I won't get into the many ways of making money (there are plenty of books that help with that). This book is about the limitations that society puts on us, and how to break the chains.

To change your mindset, you have to become a new person. I'm on my seventh identity in this life alone. I've been so many versions of myself. I've been a poor version, a single-mother version, a hood version, a nine-to-five slave version, a businesswoman version, and so many others. Each time I evolved as a person, I developed a new mindset. In the beginning, I didn't develop high-level versions of myself. But now, baby, I change my mindset for the better. The information I put in my brain is very strategic, and I try to flush bullshit out very quickly.

A poor mindset will always be just that until you change it. Start with small things, like not complaining about gas prices. I listened to an interview between the motivational speaker Eric Thomas and my favorite podcaster Tom Bilyeu. Eric Thomas said so many dope things during the interview, but one comment in particular stood out to me: "Let the gas go up! I'm going to make more money." That's a wealthy mindset right there. Why care about gas prices? You're breathing, you have a car, money still exists, and you have places to go, so trust and believe that you will have enough money to get some gas. If prices go up, then it's time to make more money! It's time to change with the universe. More is always available here. Don't get stuck in the poor mindset of inflation, recession, and gas prices. When you are on a money vibration, prices going up should excite you. That just means it's time for you to get better!

It's these small mindset shifts that put you on the vibration of the rich. A lot of poor people say things like, "Rich people are evil," and, "It's a dark world where the rich reside." I believe they say these things because they are too afraid to be rich. The idea of learning something new makes a lot of people uncomfortable. Many people don't know what having an abundance of money feels like, so it makes them uncomfortable. So they say things like, "The rich are evil."

There is nothing evil about desiring and getting everything you want from this life. You deserve the big house, the nice car, and the luxury to travel and live how you want, whenever you want. That's not evil, that's enjoying the material part of life that was given to you by those who came before us. The people before us created this luxury for all humankind, not just the rich. But if only the rich think they deserve the best, then that's the only group who will have it. You get what you think about, and thoughts really do become things. So if nothing else, stop the poor talk in your mind. You have enough money for gas, and if you don't, you need to level up. That's not the fault of the gas stations, the government, or society. That's all on you, and it's time for you to evolve.

Relationships

THE THIRD THING THAT SEPARATES THE RICH FROM THE POOR IS RELATIONSHIPS. How you treat people is what your reputation will be known as. Building good relationships and networks is a must to become the highest version of yourself. A wealthy mindset handles relationships completely differently than a poor mindset does. It's all about what both parties can do for each other in a business sense without drama or emotions, which is the complete opposite of those with a poor mindset, who only look at relationships from a sentimental standpoint.

How many of your current relationships make you money or provide you with money-making ideas? Of course, you should have normal relationships with your parents, kids, mate, etc. I'm speaking of knowing whom you spend the majority of your time with outside of your family. How are you investing in these relationships? My best friend and I don't make money together; however, we are both business owners and we discuss money-making ideas for our businesses. My soulmate and I make plenty of money together. I have real estate friends who invite me to functions that put me in the room with many other moneymakers. Relationships get built and money gets made.

I'm not trying to convince everyone to strive to be rich. But most of the population is struggling with money. There are things I've learned along the way and I'm just sharing them with you. I want us all to be great. I want us all to overcome society's standards. I want us all to know we deserve the best just like anybody else. If it's on this planet, it's available, and it's time we put our hands in the pot.

There Are Two Groups Of People On The Internet

Group one: *the consumers*

Group two: *the sellers*

ONLINE YOU ARE EITHER BUYING OR SELLING. Sadly the majority of people are buying. That must change. We must become sellers. Some of us that started with a harsh upbringing didn't have much, so stunting feels like an accomplishment. We buy a bunch of unnecessary material items before we even have the money to spend on them. Most of us are emotional spenders. We get sad and spend money, we feel overworked and spend money, we get cheated on and spend money. Meanwhile, the sellers get richer and richer.

We do live in a material universe, so you deserve all the things you want. By no means am I saying you aren't worthy enough to purchase a Chanel bag or a pair of Gucci shoes. I'm just saying you shouldn't buy those things until you have enough money that purchasing those big items won't be missed from your bank account. We must build the bag, not blow the bag. Keep manifesting in your mind and building up your wealth. You don't have to run to Amazon or Walmart every time you get paid. Use that money to invest in something that can make you more money.

I've talked about money in different forms throughout this chapter. I'm giving you the whole truth, but it's not meant to be contradictory. The biggest part is you can have whatever you want from the game of life, BUT you must play SMART! The universe will give you more money than you can spend, but only if you are aligned with how to handle that much money.

The only reason you are not wealthy yet is because you are not thinking like a wealthy person, so you are not on the vibration of abundance. If you are thinking like a consumer, you will stay broke; no matter how much money you pray or beg God for, you'll still be broke. Again, it's the reason why broke people win the lottery and become broke again. You have to change the way you think, and life will reflect back to you what you think you are worth.

I'm not a millionaire yet, but I know why. I could've been a millionaire based on the amount of money that touched my hands over the years, but I was a consumer, not a seller. As soon as I made money, I spent it. I loved showing off. I also wasn't thinking like a millionaire. Now I do! I ask myself before I purchase or do certain things, "Would a millionaire do that?" If the answer is "no" I don't do it. That's called raising your vibration. You have to become who you want to be in your mind first, then start living like that version of yourself, and it will become you. You must do it every day, along with applying action. Please stop getting paid and giving all your money to big companies. Pay yourself.

You Are Holding My Millions

THIS BOOK YOU ARE HOLDING or listening to is what officially made me a millionaire. For me, this book was never about making money, but I always intended to reach a million hearts. I'm manifesting that my words will somehow impact a million people and it will be true. This is my eighth book and it's the one. Every ounce of my being will make that statement true with energy and action. I'm so happy you are a part of this millionaire journey.

Typing those words felt so good and instantly raised my energy. I felt the abundance in my soul and I feel so connected to you. It's not weird that I feel connected to you because I'm typing these words and you are reading them, so we are on the same energy at the same time. Maybe you are reading this book years from now, but you are still with me at this moment.

The point of telling these stories is to point out that I'm not what society said I would be, and neither is money. It flows to us abundantly and I haven't felt lack since the day I changed my mindset. Simply put: Money does grow on trees, but you have to water the roots.

10

We Are More Than Our Five Senses

"We live on the leash of our senses."

~ Diane Ackerman

Physical Senses

WHAT DO YOU SMELL RIGHT NOW? What do you hear? What is the taste in your mouth? How does the paper feel as you hold this book, or the plastic if you are reading on a tablet? Lastly, acknowledge that your eyes are reading these words, right now, or perhaps your ears are listening. Our senses are available for one reason and one reason only: to interpret this reality. Society taught us that these senses are all we have. The truth is there is a vibrational reality. It's what you can't see, hear, smell, taste, or touch until it is manifested. I don't want to get too deep into this other reality – I will save that for another book – but what I will break down is how to start using your vibrational senses.

We are living in a vibrational universe, and that cannot be disputed. Everything is moving all the time. Pause a moment to take that in. Let me repeat myself: Everything is vibrating all the time. In the same way you can't use your physical senses to feel or see the vibration, is the same way you can't use your physical senses to see your vibrational reality coming into place, either. Remember how I said we came to play the game however we wanted? Well, there is help to guide you in the way you play. It's the spiritual power of the game. Every game has a card that gives you an advantage. Well, our advantage in our game is the power to believe it before your physical senses can see it, hear it, smell it, or touch it. It's the power of your subconscious mind, the power of God, the power of infinite intelligence, and the power of your inner being.

Spiritual Faith Of The Game

THE SPIRITUAL POWER OF THE GAME SHOULD NOT BE IGNORED. It should be used constantly to see results. Trying to figure out life using only your five senses will keep you average at best. That means you would only believe what you can see, touch, or feel. If everyone thought that way, we wouldn't have anything we can see, touch, or feel because no one would have used their spiritual power to imagine and believe before they could see it. It's very important to use this benefit of the game. You have to believe that whatever you want can be provided for you BEFORE seeing it. In order to believe, you must feel it—you can't fake it or trick the game into thinking you believe. Since we are in a vibrational universe, your vibration must match your desires. You must not look for proof that your desire can be achieved; you must just know.

Just knowing is where faith comes in. Faith is rarely talked about, but it is so instrumental to life. It is the key that opens many doors, it's the missing piece to many puzzles, and it's the answer to many problems. Good ole faith. After you believe you can have whatever you want, you then need to have the faith to allow it to happen. We use faith all the time without noticing it.

When you walk out the door of your home, you have faith that you will walk back through that same door. But how? No one promised you that you would live through the day. You couldn't see yourself in the evening walking through the door. You had to believe you would return home, and you used faith without even knowing it. Faith does not use your five senses. Faith is strictly used in the spiritual world. No matter whom you serve, what your religion is, where you come from, or how hard life has been for you, using faith will work every time.

Vibrational Senses

Let's talk about what I want at this very moment. I said I can have whatever I want in the game, right? Well, right now, I want a detox smoothie. That's what I want. I can't physically see it in front of my face, I can't smell it at this very moment, I can't touch it, I can't taste it on my tongue, BUT I believe I can have it. Thoughts become things. My vibrational senses already know the smoothie exists, and it will send me the thoughts to get the desire I want. My faith knows I can have whatever I want.

The Process of Vibrational Senses

1. I want a smoothie (my desire)

2. I have to believe either I can have it or I can't (my belief)

3. Thoughts tell me how to get a smoothie (spiritual power, my subconscious, my guidance system, knowledge)

4. I listen to the thoughts and start the journey to getting a smoothie (action, faith)

5. Smoothie manifests (the universe, God, higher power, faith)

So the moment the thought crossed my mind, everything started working to get me a smoothie. I didn't use any of my physical senses to think about a smoothie before I could see it. So how did the thought become a thing? The universe gave me options.

Here are some options

- I could drive to the smoothie place.

- I could use Uber eats.

- I could walk two miles to the smoothie place.

- I could make my own smoothie.

- I could go to the market and get the ingredients.

- I could use a delivery service and someone could bring me the ingredients.

The vibrational reality is so cool because it already has people who woke up to go to work to make smoothies for us. So I can drive in my car, get out, order a smoothie, wait while someone makes it, pay for it, and then take my first sip. Yes, this is just a simple analogy about a smoothie, but it works that way for everything you want in your life.

Don't take your physical senses so seriously. You have to believe in what you DON'T see just as much as what you DO see, or it can't manifest. If you want more money, believe it before you see or touch it. If you want a new mate, believe it before you can actually feel that person physically. The vibrational reality works for you. It's trying to guide you toward what you want.

Our physical senses are beautiful and I love all five of them, but they would not hold any value without our spiritual senses to guide us along the easiest path to our desires. I want you to believe as deeply in this spiritual power as you believe in the wind. You can't see the wind, but you can feel it. It's blowing and hitting your skin like an invisible power. That is the exact same power the universe has to guide you to all of your desires.

STORYTIME

SUNNI T. CONNOR

"Homeless in California"

When I was young I daydreamed about moving out of Baltimore. I just wanted to see what the world had to offer. My first traveling experience was riding to South Carolina with my grandfather and cousins to see family. I loved the open road and driving through multiple states. I knew then that I wanted to live somewhere else.

Atlanta was the second state I visited when I was about thirteen, and I fell in love with the Southern hospitality. I couldn't believe people were that nice and welcoming. Everyone greeted each other, and it was respectful to say "Good morning." By the end of the trip, I was happily walking into each establishment loudly saying, "Good morning." The kindness of the people felt right.

I made up my mind that I would leave my home town. I would live in a place where I could be my true self. I didn't know where that place was at the time. After many failed attempts to leave Maryland, I finally left and moved to California.

I came to California with two suitcases, my soulmate, my two children, and no house. We lived in a hotel for three months and spent over ten thousand dollars before we found a place.

Why do I tell this story? Because my five senses couldn't predict the unknown of moving here. I couldn't smell a house before we hopped on a plane. I couldn't taste what our future would be like in California. I couldn't hear what kind of car I would drive, I couldn't feel the color of my new furniture, and I couldn't see what life would be like in this new place. My five senses didn't work in the unknown. I had to use faith, intuition, the Law of Attraction, and the power of the universe. I had to believe. I had no guarantees that anything would work out. My five senses helped me interpret the new state, but it was the power of the universal senses that aligned everything.

My soulmate and I looked at places just about every day. I was a picky homeless chick. Some of the places were too small or didn't accept pets (I love my dog like one of my children), some of them weren't in a good school district, and some of them had twenty other people applying to the same place. Although we were staying in a hotel, by this time I had mastered manifesting my desires. The universe had shown me too many times how to ask, believe, and prepare for whatever I wanted.

After many failed attempts at finding a place, something magical happened. I meditated that morning and I heard the special voice say, "Stop stressing. You will be out of the hotel by the end of the week." I listened to it and I released all my worries.

Later that day we were driving on the highway and I kept seeing mattresses everywhere. They were tied to the tops of people's cars and one had even fallen off in the middle of the highway. I told my soulmate, "The universe is showing us it's time to buy a bed." He laughed and said, "We don't even have a house." We kept driving and I saw more and more beds, and I pointed them out to him. He found it strange as well, so he let me talk him into driving to the mattress store.

We purchased a mattress and a bedroom set that day, and the guy at the furniture store asked, "Where should I deliver the new set?" I told him, "I don't know. We don't have an address yet, but we will have one by the end of the week." He gave me a weird look and told me to call him with an address when I had one. The next morning we were approved for the perfect place. It was in a very convenient location, a gated community with all the amenities I wanted, as well as some extras like a hot tub. I loved the school district, and it has been such a pleasure living here. Every single thing I wanted in a house, we now have.

Our spiritual senses not only gave us the life of our dreams, but they're the only things that could help us navigate the unknown. The magic is in the unknown. Faith is believing before you see it. Your higher self is pulling you closer to your desires, but you still have to go. You have to jump and know the parachute will open. You have to tap into the sixth sense, which I call your spiritual guidance, your special voice, your inner being, your higher self. Your sixth sense is the invisible power you came here with. Don't live this life not using it, or you will never take those jumps that can enhance your life for the better.

Universal Senses

BEFORE I DIVE DEEP INTO THE TOPIC OF UNIVERSAL SENSES, let's talk about the captain riding the ship.

Captain = Your spirit

Ship = Your body

You are not the ship (*your body*)—you are the captain (*your spirit*). Although they are together and it takes both to travel the ocean, the captain is not the ship. The ship takes directions from the captain and the captain takes directions from the universe. Anytime the captain doesn't take directions from the universe, the ship *(your mind and body)* gets lost as well.

Just like your five senses, there are universal senses. These senses are all about what you feel. I've never heard of the term *universal senses*, but I know they exist. I just did a quick Google search, and yeah, no one is talking about universal senses, so we just entered into a new world.

How they work is simple. They are the complete opposite of your physical senses. You can't see what the universe is doing for you until it's done. You can't touch the manifestations until they've materialized. It's an amazing feeling, tapping into the universal senses before the desired manifestation occurs.

Universal Sense #1

Imagination

THE EASIEST WAY TO USE YOUR IMAGINATION IS TO VISUALLY THINK ABOUT the version of yourself you want to be. Feel how it feels to be whatever you want. If you want to be an actor, use your imagination to walk on the stage and accept your Oscar, then use your feeling of excitement as if it's really happening. You can't just think about it—you must also feel it. Get pumped up to be an award-winning actor. Plan out your speech and say it in your mind. Thank God for allowing you to come so far. Do all of this before it happens. It puts you on the frequency of an Oscar-winning actor.

Universal Sense #2

Invisibility

THE UNIVERSE IS AN INVISIBLE FORCE OF POWER, AND IT'S ALL ABOUT WELL-BEING. Let's imagine you stop at a stop sign, and after checking both ways, you drive through. Then, out of nowhere, a car runs the stop sign and comes to a screeching halt seconds before hitting you. That's the kind of invisible universal power I'm talking about. Now it could've been an angel that saved you, but I don't know much about angels so I won't get into that, but whatever it was, you couldn't see it and it was working for the universe.

It's important that you allow this universal sense, because most of what you want is invisible right now. Unlike imagination, with which you can tap into a universal sense by creating a picture in your mind, this one is all on the universe. It quietly gets everything done, but your job is just to believe. Believe you are protected from the car that's going to run the stop sign, believe your fancy house exists, and believe you can have whatever you want.

Universal Sense #3

Alignment

THE UNIVERSE KNOWS WHAT IS ALIGNED WITH WHAT. You can't trick it or fake it. If you want something that you don't believe you can have, then you are not in alignment with that thing. If you want something that you don't match up with, then you are not in alignment with that thing.

Let's say a man wants a wife who cooks, cleans, works, and takes care of the children he has with another woman, but he doesn't want her to have any children of her own. What vibration is that kind of woman on? She would have to be a single woman, a submissive woman, maybe a woman who can't birth children of her own, a woman looking to be married, a woman who enjoys cooking and caring for the household, and a woman who works well under pressure, since she'll be working too.

Now, let's say that particular man wants all of that out of her, but he doesn't have an income. He sits at home all day and plays video games. I understand that may be his desire. However, he's not aligned with that kind of woman. That kind of woman desires a man who can match her energy.

"But Sunni," I can hear you say, "good women take care of men all the time." I'm not saying that a man couldn't get a woman like that in his experience. I'm saying it won't work. It's not aligned. Because we are creating our own reality, the universe allows us to make our own choices, but when we make choices WITHOUT the universe, life is a mess. When we make choices WITH the universe, life unfolds beautifully. You have no idea how beautiful it can be.

Now, let's go back to the woman we were talking about. You may be thinking, "How did a video-game-playing, sitting-around-the-house-eating-all-day, lazy, unmotivated man get such a woman?" There's only one answer. It's because vibrations must match, so she must have wanted someone like that. *Why would she want someone like that?* Because she has her own insecurities, or maybe her mother dated men like that and that's all she knows; maybe she never felt needed as a child, so she likes caring for her men; maybe she's extremely jealous; maybe she fears other women will take her man, but she won't have to worry about being cheated on if he stays at home all day; maybe she fell in love with his sex before knowing he didn't have a job. The possibilities are endless, but there's only one way a man like that could get a woman like that. They both must want that, whether they admit it or not. They are aligned.

Use this exact scenario but with a man who's motivated, financially stable, and ambitious. He would get that same woman and marry her. They would build a beautiful life together because they would be universally aligned. They would be on the same vibration. The PlayStation guy could get the woman, too, but they wouldn't be on the same vibration; it would be messy and they would eventually break up, and as soon as she gained her confidence, the universe would bring her Mr. Ambitious.

It must align—it is the law. Sadly, this is the reason why some rich athletes leave their high school sweethearts. They reach a different vibration once they make it, and sometimes it's easier to deal with a new girl who knows the industry than the old girl who still thinks the way she did when they were in the hood. His old girlfriend is on a much lower frequency. Is it fair to ditch the girl who held him down before he made it? Probably not, but they are no longer aligned. Also, the universe is not emotional. Being emotional is a human characteristic. Frequencies must match, fair or not.

Now, I'll be right back. I'm going to get myself a smoothie because I thought about it and I can have it. See you in the next chapter!

11

It's Only You

*"*R*emind yourself, nobody's built like you. You design yourself."*

~ Jay Z

There's No Other Option

WELP, YOU ARE STUCK WITH YOURSELF FOR ETER-
NITY. There's only you. That's it! Just you! It took me
quite some time to realize I was all I truly had. It wasn't
that I didn't have family or support. My thoughts in
my mind would be with me every single day, and how
dare I criticize and torture the person I am instead
of loving every form of myself. I stopped comparing
myself to others on this very normal but special day.

STORYTIME

"The Bluebird"

I sat on a bench at the lake as I daydreamed about my
life. A bluebird flew up and sat on the branch of a
tree close by. As I listened to the bird's soft melody,
staring intensely into its eyes, I suddenly realized the
bird was also living in a reality. The bird was also living
an experience.

I wondered if a bluebird calls the color "blue" blue?
Do other realities recognize color? Do birds have

fears? Does a bird ever stop and wonder if its wings will properly open when it takes a leap off a high tree, or does it just have faith that it won't fall flat and die? As I sat there daydreaming about this bird, another bird flew up. The other bird was dark brown. It was bland, with hardly any design or uniqueness. The bluebird then flew to a different branch and continued to sing. My question to you is, did the brown bird look at the beautiful bluebird and say, "I sure wish I was born with some color like you. I'm brown and plain. I'm the color of poop. I hate this life. If only I was born blue." I seriously doubt it. Don't you ever look at another person and wish you had anything they have. You have what you have, and what you have is good.

There is no comparison! There is no other person better than you, prettier than you, sexier than you, or smarter than you. The reason why is that you are in your own reality. You are not inside anyone else's mind. You are just with you. Your thoughts about "you" are all that matters. Don't worry about what society says is normal. In your mind, you can be a bluebird or a brown bird, but by no means does either color define you. No one else's appearance matters.

What the others have doesn't matter. What they think in their own minds doesn't matter. Only you matter. When those people go on about their day, you will not be a thought in their minds. They live in their own reality as well.

I once compared myself to others. Not in an envious way but in an admirable way. I admired what I saw in others, which always left me wishing I had more. The problem with this way of thinking is you often start beating yourself up for everything that is wrong with you. You start thinking about how much further you would be in life had you just finished college, or left home sooner, or gotten that tummy tuck. There is no comparison. You can learn from others, but to truly learn anything you must experience it. Otherwise, you haven't learned—you've just received more information.

Be Selfish

SOME PEOPLE MAY STRONGLY DISAGREE WITH WHAT I'M ABOUT TO SUGGEST. I can feel the guilt overwhelming some just by reading such thoughts. Well, I'm sorry, but this is something everyone needs to know. BE SELFISH! That's right. Put yourself first at all times. You come before ANYONE else, and that includes your spouse, family, and even your children. We have been lied to again. Society teaches us that we must do for others first, which is a huge reason we are all so screwed up.

I was one of the most giving people many people knew. I would give to everyone before myself, even to strangers. I tried to make everyone else happy before I pleased myself, and it felt normal to put others first. I figured that if I gave, I would always be blessed. I didn't do it for the blessing, though; I just felt it was what I should do.

That all changed one day as I was sitting on an airplane next to my children, waiting for instructions from the flight attendant. Suddenly, something beautiful happened. An attractive young flight attendant with an exotic look stood in the middle of the plane with a life vest around her body. She gave one specific instruction that changed my entire outlook on being selfish. She said, "In case of an emergency landing or if the aircraft loses ventilation, grab your face mask from the drop-down bin over your head and place it on your face. If you have small children, place it on their face ONLY after you have put your oxygen mask on first."

Wow, that moment still gives me the chills. I took those words to mean that I must provide oxygen for myself first before I have the strength to help someone else. I can't help my children if I can't breathe. I felt guilty at first. It didn't seem fair to put my mask on so I could get air before my children did. It's actually more than fair, though, to replenish my lungs before I help them. If I gave them a mask first, I would die by the time I got to myself, but if I got to myself first I would have the strength to rapidly provide them with oxygen. Always make sure you are breathing first. Before you consider anyone else, consider yourself first and how the situation makes you feel. You were created as a single human. It is your highest responsibility to care for your spirit before anyone else, or you are doing your inner being a great disservice.

Benefits Of Being Selfish

WHAT HAPPENS WHEN YOU BECOME SELFISH? You actually can do more for those who deserve it. Initially, friends will drop like flies. You will realize they were only in your life for what you could do for them. They needed to be dismissed anyway. The next set of people will adjust, and lastly, the people who truly love you will actually get more out of you. Let me put it this way:, If you always make sure you are happy first, then everyone around you will be happy.

I feel I need to explain more, so let me give you a visual analogy. Let's say your mother-in-law is having a party at her house. You are usually the person who runs around getting everything others don't feel like getting. Usually you do it with no complaints, but it makes you feel horrible on the inside. You are tired of being the person everyone takes advantage of, but you keep playing that role anyway.

Well, on this particular day, you want to show up to your mother-in-law's party with a bottle of wine like all the other guests. You had a day planned to pamper yourself before the party. At the last minute, your mother-in-law calls asking for a number of different things for you to pick up before the party, but you are already on your way to the hair salon. What are the options? Tell her no, and have her upset with you the entire night? Should you cancel your appointment and run her errands for her party? Ask your husband if he can do it, so your mother-in-law won't be upset? Say no, don't think about it, and continue on with your day? The last option sounds rude, huh?

Well, it's her party! Any other option is not your problem. It's okay to say, "No." Let me tell you what would have happened if you had canceled your pamper time to please your mother-in-law. You would have been miserable. You would have complained the entire day, thinking, *Why did she ask me? Why didn't she pick up her own fruit? What am I going to do with my hair now?* You would have run her errands for her party, and by the time you arrived as a guest, you would have been irritated, not to mention how messed up your hair would have been. It would have meant choosing her happiness over your own. She's twirling around with her beautiful host dress, nice nails, and freshly done hair while you are sitting there irritated because you did nothing for yourself that day. I could've picked a better or more serious analogy. I chose a simple one like this to make my point. It doesn't matter what the circumstances are—you must ALWAYS please yourself first, and the party will go on!

Learn to say, "NO," and then don't think about it. Move right along with your day. Remind yourself, that "YES" for them is "NO" for me. If they are upset with you, that is not your issue. They must deal with their own emotions. So pull up with your bottle of wine and enjoy the party like the other guests. Every day you wake up, the goal is to feel good, and nothing is to interfere with that goal.

Be Unique

"PICTURE PUZZLES ARE MADE OF MANY PIECES. They all fit together to form a big picture. What would happen if one of those pieces was not the shape it was meant to be?" — Bashar

I love this quote. I take it to mean that we should be the unique shapes we were designed to be so that we can fit the puzzle as a whole. We should never try to be someone else, or else we are leaving our space on the puzzle empty. Together we make a beautiful picture, but we must be our own unique piece.

As people, we tend to follow or copy others. It serves us no purpose to want to be like other people unless they share the same passion as we do. If they do, we can admire them but we should still bring our own creativity to the idea. We are just as special. Imagine how hard the universe must work to give us what we want while we are acting like someone else. It's almost impossible to give you someone else's desires. It has to emotionally mean something to you, not just because someone else has it.

Think about this: There are many components to a hit song. It requires a catchy beat, a nice harmony, an artist, a mixer, a studio, a sound engineer, sometimes a ghostwriter, equipment, radio stations, and much more. Imagine if you are the artist and your role is to sing, but you want to play all the roles. Of course, that is possible because humans can duplicate many talents. However, you are not likely to have a hit song. There are many other pieces (people) on the puzzle that have the perfect talent to make the song magical. Chill out and let other people in the universe help you manifest your dreams. Be unique—don't try to be everybody.

We can only be us. Here's a secret, and I want you to write this somewhere and keep it close. Say it out loud: "Being unique is the answer to my success." That's the real secret. Look at any famous superstar and tell me if they acted exactly like someone else. There will never be another Michael Jackson, Denzel Washington, Elvis Presley, Michael Jordan, and so on. There will be other people who share their same passions, but they won't ever be exactly them.

Kobe Bryant really admired Michael Jordan, and he started his career modeling his style. Kobe didn't fully become the superstar he was until he became, "Kobe Bryant!" Some have even said he was better than Michael. The fact that he can be mentioned in the same sentence as his idol showed his hard work and dedication to his passion. But he too had a special piece in the puzzle, which is why his uniqueness took him far in the NBA. Which is also why the game ended for him when it did. He was so unique that even his death became part of his legacy.

There is no duplication in this universe. You will live and die on the terms of the game. You can't be another player no matter how hard you try. There's only YOU! Watch how your life takes off when you become who you really are.

I actually never wanted to be anyone else. However, there were times I felt like I didn't know who I was. I did what I thought was expected of me. I acted how I thought an author should act. I tried to be the perfect mother like the women in the movies. I couldn't get to my greatness because I wasn't being one hundred percent myself.

I'm actually an outcast, a misfit, some would even say crazy, and boy do I love it! I never want to fit in with society again. I love being a misfit. I love living *my life* my way. Fuck being validated by other boring assholes! I get to be "Me" and I'm pretty amazing. When I used to fit in with everyone else, I was bored, broke, and miserable. Not fitting in is working pretty damn well for me, I must say. It's imperative that you get to know yourself. Like really know yourself. Not what's expected of you, but what you really want. Take some time and really think about what would make you happy. You are ultimately stuck with yourself for eternity! Not just this lifetime, because you'll be with your soul forever. Give it what it wants, and watch your life become fulfilled. That's a fact!

Mind Your Business

WHAT OTHER PEOPLE ARE DOING IS NOT YOUR CONCERN. Don't waste energy on watching others live their lives. Start living your life. Use your time wisely. The time you waste worrying about what someone else is doing is time you could've been working on your dreams. Lost time is not gained. Once it's gone, it's gone.

No one is in that brain of yours but you. Only you. That should be your main focus. Now, am I saying you should never talk to another human again, or not care about your family? Of course not. I'm speaking about how realizing it's all in your mind helps you create the life you want, which includes having the people you want in it.

It's really your world. Sometimes that's hard to understand, but you are living in a dimension of the universe that's built solely on your experience. You are not living someone else's reality. Only yours. So mind your business and focus on your experience.

This Is Your World

EVERYTHING IN YOUR LIFE IS SHOWING YOU A REALITY THAT YOU CHOSE FROM THOUGHTS IN

YOUR MIND. You chose your spouse, your house, your job, whether or not to have kids. You chose to be clean or dirty, busy or lazy, greedy or content with only what your body needed. You chose to break the law or hang with people who did, or you chose to walk a straight path. You are the boss of your experience. It's you! I have to repeat that so it really sinks in. Your entire life is what you have created it to be.

You are the one in control—there are no excuses. Start acting like it. Start doing what you want to do and how you want to do it. If you are unhappy in your relationship, LEAVE. Get out! Don't make excuses like, "We have a family together." "I need help with these bills." "My kids need him around." Those kinds of thoughts are your ego lying to you to keep you comfortable. It's really uncomfortable, starting over or leaving someone you've been with for years. Being uncomfortable is where the power is. If you are afraid to be uncomfortable, that's fine, but just know you are creating your reality and causing your own misery.

I break all the rules! Society told me so much crap I had to do that my higher self didn't want to do. For example, I was told authors won't be successful if they switch genres. Guess what? I've switched from writing nonfiction memoirs to suspense to fiction, then to nonfiction self-help. I can do whatever I want. If I'd listened to society, you wouldn't be holding this book right now.

I mind my business. I don't care what anyone else is doing. I don't care what other authors are writing or how they are promoting their work. I can learn from them, but at the end of the day I have to focus on what I'm doing. If I focus on what others are doing all day, where would I get the time to "do me"? Remember the story I told at the beginning of this chapter? I told you about the two birds and how they didn't compare themselves to other birds. Well, I never told you the end of the story. It was pretty simple. The brown bird flew away and the bluebird kept singing and minding his business.

Ok, babies, this chapter is coming to an end. I just needed to remind you that you are "YOU." I do what I want to do, and today I want to be a bluebird.

12

Death Was Always The Ending

"Death is not the greatest loss in life. The greatest loss is what dies inside while still alive. Never surrender."

~ Tupac Shakur

The One Fact Of Life

THE ONE FACT THAT LIFE GIVES US FROM THE VERY BEGINNING IS DEATH. It tells us right away that we will leave this experience one day, and no one is exempt. The game must stop at some point, and death is always the end.

I want you to read this chapter like your life depends on it, because it does. I want you to never forget the words I'm providing you at this moment. You are actually here with me as I portray the images in my mind to best describe the death experience. Let's go back to the first chapter where I described the game of life and how we signed up to come here for the experience. I mentioned how we knew the ending chapter would always be death. Well, we are almost at the end of our chapters together in this book, so we must address death. I've experienced a lot of death. I've experienced enough death to be somewhat of a life expert on this chapter.

I've also grieved many different times but felt different each time. When someone dies, their spirit leaves their body and it feels like our world is about to crumble. We think of how we will miss them and how we will never see them again and how life will never be the same without them. What we never think about is the reality that there was never another option. Death is the one FACT that comes with life. Read that last sentence again, please. We were never promised eternity here, and frankly, I don't think your spirit wants to be here that long. What we must never forget is that we are here for a short time to live an experience. We are visitors, and this was never meant to be our home. Some people visit this game for a year or two, and some stay for eighty years, but it's never home either way. This vibrational reality will never be your home, which is why stressing is almost ridiculous when you remember that nothing is permanent.

The people who died before us just exited the experience before we will. We are going to leave as well, and we need not fear the end but instead embrace the day that our spirit jumps out of this beautiful body. Your body allows your spirit to connect with it, use it, and sometimes abuse it, and yet it still tries to hang in there to keep you healthy.

Your body is a small piece of the puzzle. You should focus ninety percent on your spirit. Get to know yourself. You came here with the spirit, and if nothing else you will leave here with that same spirit, so work on being the best you can ever be. If you don't get to know yourself, you will have wasted a big part of your life.

You Are The Instructor

TAKE A DEEP BREATH. Let it out slowly, then say, "That is me breathing." Now instruct your big toe to lift up; actually say it out loud. Now acknowledge, "That is me telling my toes to move." Lastly, smell your arm, then say, "That is me smelling my arm." You are someone. You are so special, and at this very second, you are alive. But, the person who just instructed you to do those things will always be alive. That is you. That is you when your precious body is six feet under, that is you when you are sick, and that is you when you are tired. That voice won't die. You came here with that voice. Even if you haven't listened to anything I've said so far, please get to know that voice. That is your eternal spirit. Your spirit will never die; your experience will just end. That's why it is so important to know and love yourself, because you are an eternal being living a temporary experience.

The universe is perfect, and so is death. I know it seems unfair, especially when the people we love leave the game. We must remember that they never intended to stay. We will miss them, we will cry and reminisce, but we have to always keep living while we are here. I've lost people who held a big piece of my heart, and they were also part of my everyday experience. I've grieved so hard that once I lost over fifteen pounds from stress. I've lost hair, weight, and even my insanity at one point. So no, I'm not saying you shouldn't grieve or that we should all handle death well. I'm saying it's important to recognize that death is simply the end of a game we never intended to play forever. Nothing more, nothing less. It's the same ending we were aware of the day we were born.

Don't Fear Death

SOCIETY HAS PROGRAMMED US TO FEAR DEATH, hide from it, and mourn it for years. But if death consumes us, are we really living? What if we never listened to society's bullshit programs? What if death was celebrated? What if we knew we would never see our loved ones again, but we were happy that they lived one hell of a life? They left their mark behind for others to enjoy. What if we celebrated their bold characters and smiled at the good times we had with them? What if we just kept playing the game and appreciated that those people got to be part of our experience? Of course, it would still hurt, but we always knew it was coming one day.

Let's die together right now (in our minds). I'm walking through a dirt-filled cemetery and I see a tombstone that says, "Sunni T. Connor, a loving mother, bestselling author, motivational speaker; a giver, a lover, and an adventurer." What would yours say? Picture it right now. What mark did you leave here? My spirit won't be sad that I had to leave this planet, because I did everything I wanted to do. I'm doing everything I want to do every day, and there's not a day that goes by that I'm not living my life exactly as I want. Live exactly as you want and the end will have value because you came here and followed your purpose.

Suicidal Thoughts

BEFORE I START ON THIS TOPIC, if anyone is having suicidal thoughts at this moment please call the suicide hotline, a supportive friend, or a family member.

I must address these thoughts that are kept so quiet. Life can be hard, and many if not all of us have thought about ending the experience. At the time of pain, it feels like the easiest option to just end it all. That would be the wrong choice. We discussed choices in Chapter Four. Life is a choice that you must keep choosing. You have no idea how great your life can be until you apply the changes you need.

Maybe I can come off like I have it all figured out, but I don't. No one does. Only this morning, a suicidal thought crossed my mind. I woke up feeling down, uninspired, and hopeless. I felt like I was breaking and no one had the pieces to put me back together. Only I hold the pieces to my masterpiece. Feeling down today was exhausting, and it was hard for me to snap back.

With all this advice in this book, it's important to know that not every day will be a good day, no matter what knowledge you have. But if you don't let the enemy in your mind convince you that dying is the way out of your pain, then you are still a valuable player in the game. We talked about thoughts in Chapter Five and how some of them are not *your* thoughts, and I can ensure you that if you are thinking about suicide, that's not the **real** you. The *real you's* entire existence is to keep you alive, not to talk you into dying.

As I mentioned earlier, I was stressed when the thought to end it all crossed my mind, but today is just a day and it was just a thought. That's it. It was one horrible day. I get to go to sleep tonight and wake up and start over. The game goes on. Nothing and no one is taking me out of this experience. I will wake up and say, "Forget about everything!" Even speaking about it now, I can't believe I let petty issues stress me out. Now I feel much better and I'm laughing at the thought of leaving this experience. Now keep in mind, I made a choice. I could've fallen into a deeper depression, I could've kept replaying an old story, I could've become a victim, or I could've convinced myself I don't belong here anymore. I chose the best choice for me, which was to simply take a nap. When I woke up, I started writing this chapter. I used my restart button.

These bad days are blessings, and the tears I cried are my strength. I'm sharing this with you because there is no perfect life, but you can make a flawed life worth living. Because even when you feel at your lowest, you are still being yourself. Family and friends want you to put on a fake smile to make them feel comfortable, but you must be true to yourself. My truth today was I felt like shit, but now I'm grateful. I'm grateful I allowed myself to experience feeling low, because now I feel so good.

There are no mistakes, only lessons. However, suicide would be a mistake because you would no longer be here to play. A person who ends their own experience allows demonic thoughts to win. I learned a lot today by being in this unusual dark space. I first learned I want to live more than anything else. So that means whatever is going on can't be bigger than my existence. I then learned my low energy affected the people in my house tremendously, because I couldn't pretend to be happy even for them. Lastly, I learned that if I just get back to putting myself first, I feel much better. Please keep in mind that the suicidal thought only crossed my mind once. Imagine how toxic it can be for someone to repeat a false story of hopelessness.

If you are having multiple horrible days, you have to fix the issue. Only you know the issue. If it's your toxic family or an unhealthy relationship, you may have to let it go. Perhaps it's your self-esteem or insecurities. It could be the loss of a family member. You have to use your key to open the door. Remember that fear is under your control. You have to face fear, and your power will always be on the other side of the door.

If the death of a loved one is the reason you want to give up, please know that if you were meant to die with that loved one, you would've. We've seen many times when freak accidents happen and multiple family members die together, such as in fires, airplane or car accidents, etc. That wasn't your destiny. You are here. You are now. You are worthy. You are loved, and I love you.

I have a very personal relationship with a suicidal death. My uncle committed suicide in my house when I was younger. My dad and I found him. It was horrific, and it changed me as a person. He gave up when he was only nineteen. Things would've gotten better, and things would've changed. They had to—life is always evolving. Think about when you were twelve. You can't possibly be that same person any more. You've grown mentally, physically, and emotionally. If my uncle was here now, he couldn't possibly be that nineteen-year-old boy, and those problems he was having would have passed. After years of studying and understanding life, the one fact that never changes is that we have a choice. Always choose life.

We need a plan of action when these creepy little thoughts pop into our minds. First, we must ask ourselves this: If my entire existence, including my body, is trying to keep me alive, who is trying to kill me? Knowing it's not you is enough. It doesn't matter where that thought came from—it's not you. Secondly, always remember that "this too shall pass." Go get some rest, reboot, and start over. You got this.

Instead of draining you to death about death, let's change the vibration and think about life for a moment. What do you want your life to stand for? Are you living? Are you making a difference? Will anyone know that you were here? Will you be remembered? Can you honestly say you lived to your fullest potential in this experience? Did you do what you wanted to do? Did you come here and open up doors for others to be great? Did you speak up? Did you play your game fairly and without regret? Did you follow or did you lead? I want you to know that you can change right now and start living for yourself today.

The Last Secret

HERE'S MY LAST SECRET FOR YOU: Every time you go to sleep, you die and wake up with a new start. Your thoughts are unconscious when you are resting. No matter what happened before you fell asleep, your brain will not allow life's challenges to consume you. That's why you dream. You must rest so that your thoughts can rest. Yesterday was yesterday.

You were not in control of your mind last night as you slept. Your worries and fears of whatever had happened that day were released as you dreamed. Reality died. You are not in your reality when you are asleep. If life gets too hard, do me a favor and go to sleep. I don't care what time it is—go to sleep, take a nap if you must. The restart button will be waiting for you. Believe it or not, you died last night and the universe is so freaking awesome that it woke you up today with a restart button. You don't win every move on the board of life. Sometimes you have to lose, but never give up. Your turn will come back around and you will get another chance to play.

13

The Game

"The game of life is the best game to play, but only if you acknowledge that you are playing a game."

~Sunni T. Connor

What is the game?

THE GAME IS LIFE. To live without knowing you are playing a game could be your biggest downfall. The game is the experience, and the experience is an illusion. When you die, will it still be real? Do you think your soul will be in the grave thinking, "Life was actually real," or will the experience simply be over, and therefore the illusion will be over? The game may be finished for you. However, others will still be playing until they too run out of turns.

The game never expected you to take it so seriously. It had to be real enough that you would actually experience this 3D reality, but it sent you so many signs to look for something else besides the illusion you call reality. A lot of the answers are within the sources built into the game, but we ignore the obvious. We ignore nature, the stars, and everything in the game that's flowing effortlessly. We ignore our true selves.

We become consumed with this fake version of ourselves known as the ego, which we created to help us fit into society. The game gave everyone a choice to pick a character in the beginning, and all we had to do was be him or her. But instead, we followed the masses. We followed the other players who looked like they knew what they were doing. The saddest part of all is that the person who appears to have it together the most is one step away from giving up. No one has it figured out, which is why we are supposed to just play our way. We can pick up beneficial tips and tricks along the way, but we were never supposed to separate ourselves from the source. The ego is a character we created to cope with the game. But ego is just a character; we were never supposed to take that character literally. Instead, we were supposed to focus on ourselves more.

If you are human, there is no other game to play besides life. If you decide not to play anymore, the illusion will end and your body that exists in this reality will decompose. That seems unfair, but it's not unfair if you can stay conscious enough to know you are playing a game. Most games are fun, aren't they? Why is the game of life so hard? Mainly it's because most of us aren't playing right; we literally sucked all the fun out of it by becoming insecure maniacs. We lost control of the ego. In some people their ego is so big that they can't even hear God anymore. We have to get back to us.

The game is just that, a game. It's to be played, not worried about, not stressed over, not overanalyzed, not run by fear, not run by ego, but simply played.

What Is The Program?

THE PROGRAM IS THE SYSTEM RUNNING YOUR MIND. Think of technology being linked to strings in your brain. Think of every memory as an electric shock that connects to one of the strings in your mind. Those electric shocks of energy are the beginning stages of creating your program. The strings are linked to memories and feelings about specific events. As time went on, we added more and more unnecessary information to the program, which caused us to eventually become unhappy. We began to rely on the program alone, which then made us programmed. We forgot to use our intuitive thoughts more than our programmed thoughts.

If you do anything the same way every single time, you are using a program. The program typically doesn't require you to think. It runs on autopilot. If you do everything the exact same every morning, then you are not living. That is the program living for you. The program does, however, have its benefits, because you don't want to think about every little thing, such as how to walk. Once you learned how to walk, your program remembered and now you walk without thinking. That's the point of the program: to remember the things we shouldn't have to think about, so we can use our brain power on creating new things.

The problem is that society and inexperienced humans added things to your program as well, and you stopped thinking about things that required thought. You began to rely solely on the program. It's just a tool in the game that you were supposed to use only for its intended purpose. Many of us have become lazy thinkers. I watch people run to Google to ask how to spell a word instead of sounding out the letters and trying to spell it on their own. That is lazy thinking. You can't be successful if you don't want to think. You can't play the game without thinking. You won't have strategies on how to win; you will just make each move based on the program.

We can't avoid the program altogether because it's filled with information we've accumulated since we were babies. Some information we need and some we don't. We came to the game of life with nothing, no impressions, no thoughts, and no interpretation of this place. A newborn knows nothing about anything. Everything is just empty space and there is no judgment from a newborn about life or materials. It's why a one-year-old will play with pots and pans as if they are the best toys in the world. It's not until society strips them of their imagination or their programmed mothers yell, "Don't play with those pans. Here, take this toy." That's when a baby makes the interpretation that those noisy fun pans aren't good enough, and they should instead play with a colorful, uneventful commercialized piece of plastic crap. What I love most of all is that before that child is fully controlled or programmed, he or she will always go back and play with the pots and pans again.

What's On The board?

How can you play a game without knowing what's on the board? That would be impossible. The board is the universe. It's all connected and you are part of that connection, which is why you must tap into something higher than your limited reality. Let's call outer space the part of the board most will never experience. Since we get to play the game our way, most players don't have a strong urge to visit space. However, that doesn't mean it's off limits. Some humans have enjoyed that side of the board game as well. I plan to be one of them.

Nature is a huge part of the board game. It's everywhere. Trees, plants, dirt, rivers, clouds, mountains, the Moon, and the Sun are natural substances built into the board, unlike the players who come and go. If you play this game and don't purposely include nature, you will not be playing to win. You need to show respect to the components built into the game, such as the Sun. The Sun is so beautiful. It shows up every morning to love us. In history, some worshiped the Sun as a God because without it we would die. Without the Sun, the earth would be like a hard ball of ice. Things we take for granted like food, heat, and life wouldn't exist without the Sun. The Sun has been known to help maintain strong bones, strengthen your immune system, reduce stress, help you sleep, fight off depression, and even give you a longer life. You should respect the Sun.

You can't truly avoid nature, because you will never walk outside and not see the sky, or go out on a summer day and not feel the sun blazing on your skin, or survive for years without water. Speaking of water, every time you are in the presence of water, say thank you and show respect. The universe will reward you for your gratitude. Water makes up 70% of our bodies, and peep this, it also makes up about 70% of earth's atmosphere. It's not a coincidence that our body needs the same amount of water as Earth. And if you think that is strange, let's not forget that 70% of oxygen comes from the ocean. Again, we are all connected, so much so that the percentage is the same. The energy of the water influences the behavior of the weather, climate, and much more. Water can wipe out entire cities if it so chose. Don't play this game stupidly. Respect the water.

Of course, we also have animals, insects, and many other living creatures on the board including humans. I won't discuss every single thing on the board (that would take a whole book, in and of itself), but you get the basics.

Who Are The Players?

THE CONSCIOUSNESS OF THE PLANET WORKS AS A WHOLE. Some call this source God, some call it the

Universe, Inner being, Infinity, Allah, and so many other things. The name is not as important as the energy and the understanding that all things are working together. Because this oneness is so strong, when players separate themselves from all that is, it doesn't benefit the game or the player. Which is why racism is really just about hating yourself. The hate a racist person feels towards another player is the hate that's within them. You can't grab hate out of thin air. It has to come from somewhere. Everything that's within shows outward.

So, who are the players? All of us. Every single race on this planet, along with any other living creature. We all have a place, and the game goes smoother when we work together. For example, keeping the ocean clean helps every living thing in the ocean, which in return keeps providing us with that 70% of oxygen that we so desperately need. Starting a company and only hiring people of your skin color will not result in success in the long run. We have to work together.

Walmart is owned by the Walton family, who are white. If they had started the company and decided they would only hire white people, they would not have become the global company they are today. They played with all the other players so that they could be successful. We must play nice. Most of us need to humble ourselves and recognize we all came to the games with gifts. Collaborate with others to play the game strategically and with intention. Everyone on this planet is equal. Humans somehow think they are the most important, but they are not. We need all the players to survive. Einstein believed that if all the bees died, we would only have four years left of life. That's how connected we are, that's how much we need each other. Respect all the players in this short time we have here.

What Are The Rules?

THERE ARE ONLY THREE RULES TO THE GAME:

1. To live.

2. To do you.

3. To die.

This may or may not shock you, but there aren't many rules. You were granted free will to play how you want. Although I just explained to you why you should respect nature and play fair with the other players, no rule says that if you don't, you'll immediately die. There are consequences, but those aren't the same as rules. Just like in a real game, if you cheat while playing, the other players might not want to play with you anymore (that would be the consequence of being a cheater), but there are no rules that say you can't cheat.

So if there are no rules to life, how do we know what to do while playing? That's the beauty of it: You can do whatever you want. You can be whoever you want to be. You can start thirty businesses, have ten children, run a whore house, sleep outside every day, be a murderer, use drugs, abuse alcohol, become a teacher, run for president. Anything you can think of, you can do. So now that you know you can play the game however you want, what are you waiting for?

I wouldn't recommend using your free will for evil because, as I mentioned earlier, there will be consequences. Why do bad things happen to good people? Perhaps because sometimes things are not balanced. Everyone doesn't use their free will for good, and sometimes good energy may cross paths with bad energy. That is a question I can't answer definitively because I don't have the frequency to know that answer. But what I do know is that no matter how good or bad your experiences are, they make you who you are. Although there aren't many rules to the game, there are laws of the universe that you can follow to make the game a more pleasurable experience. I spoke about the universal laws in Chapter One.

Because there are no rules, there should never be any guilt. Of course, you'll make mistakes and do things you are not proud of. It's not your fault; there were no rules. You were just playing to the best of your ability. Whatever past decision you may be ashamed of or feel guilty for, let it go. It was just an experience, and I'm sure there was a lesson to be learned and you did the best you could at that moment.

How To Play To Win?

- Understand you are playing a game.

- Pass each level and don't look back.

- Use intention and the source for guidance.

- Be unique and walk your own path.

- Have Fun!

YOU CAN PLAY HOWEVER YOU WANT. But just know that only the players who are tapping into their source will hear the guidance required to flow with life. Playing with strong intentions will always help you win. You cannot play alone and win—you must work with other gifted and talented players. You also cannot play blindly and win, which is why you need an intention. What do you want? Don't be afraid to go get it. You have an entire universe waiting for you to win. One person winning benefits us all. We all use toilet paper, but only one person invented it. Don't die and leave your gift at the grave. We need you.

The game has levels. We all had to do some dumb, reckless, irresponsible things to learn so we could reach a new level. Why feel guilty when you know there are no rules, only experiences? We are just figuring this shit out as we go. No need to be hard on ourselves. Just keep playing. There is another level waiting to be achieved, so don't dwell on a mistake from the past. Don't ever rush the game. It's not the manifestation that brings the ultimate joy, it's the journey. The fun part is getting to where you are going. Once you get there, you are there, and then it starts all over again. Rushing is how some people miss out on all the fun, because they didn't become present for the journey.

Whatever the next journey in your life is, have fun getting there. I had so much fun writing this book, and it was such an exciting journey, but there's already another book waiting to be written. That's why I didn't rush this process. I'll have fun making this a bestseller – that will be a journey – but I won't stop until it's done. Once it's done, I'll have the pleasure of what being a bestselling author feels like for only a few moments. All that work, and I'll only get a few moments of pleasure before my journey starts on a new mission.

Think of when you first get a brand new car. You can smell the material, your confidence is on one thousand, you think everyone sees you stepping out of your new whip, and the excitement is out of this world. Time passes, and one day you just jump in the car and pull off. The excitement is gone. That will always happen. Nothing can keep you happy forever. No material manifestation can make you complete. You are whole right now, without the car or the bestselling author title. So, why do we try to reach these goals? Because we are playing the game, and it's fun. How boring would life be if you had absolutely nothing to do?

What I want you to really understand is that you are already whoever you are striving to be. As I like to tell people, "You don't have to strive for what you are!" So because you are whole right now, you going after anything you desire is just you playing the game. You don't actually need anything. Don't think your desires will make you complete. Play, have fun, and know that you are already whole.

The last thing I want you to know about winning the game is that you can only win by being unique. You are the only player designed the way you are, and the moment you try to be another player you have already lost. This can't be ignored, because your gift is invaluable. Why not try to win? You will keep waking up whether you play or not. If you choose not to play, society will play for you, and that's as bad as it gets. At some point the game will be over for all of us, so why not venture out and explore all the possibilities of the game? The game itself never dies; it goes on, and new players arrive. When the new players show up, will you have left something to be remembered for? Will you have played your part? Or will you take your gift to the grave and waste an entire experience?

Final Words

FUCK YESTERDAY, FUCK SOCIETY, AND FUCK YOUR OLD STORY. You can hit that restart button every morning and be who the FUCK you want to be *unapologetically*. You can play this game however you want, and if you make a few mistakes, GOOD! At least you are playing. Living is dropping five FUCK bombs in one paragraph and not giving a FUCK... Oops, now it's six.

Remember how, in the introduction of this book, I said I was sent here to relay this message? Well, here is my final conclusion.

- We were born with a spirit that's known as our inner being. That part of you doesn't die.

- We only get to experience life for a very limited time. We can do whatever we want with this experience.

- Fear is an illusion, so face it and gain power.

- Living in the past and telling old stories will hold us back.

- Money is only energy, and it flows effortlessly.

- We have choices in the game—there is no one choosing for us.

- Don't seek attention or validation from others, but boldly be who you want to be.

- Create your own identity; don't let society do it for you.

- Protect your energy.

- Intentions help you reach your goals.

- Your five senses are only here to interpret this reality (focus on your spiritual/universal senses more).

- There's only you! Put yourself first. It will be better for others in the long run.

- You are the creator of your reality.

- Follow the laws of the universe, especially the Law of Attraction, and play to win.

- Death was always the ending for all of us, but that doesn't mean you have to be forgotten. Leave your mark on this planet. Let people know you were here.

"We are only on this planet for a little bit of time. If in that time LIFE gives you lemons, don't be sour. Instead, bite those motherfuckers!" ***Sunni T. Connor***

A Message From The Author

My intention is to help as many people as possible, which is why I made this book so affordable. If this book helped you in any way, please share it with others and leave a review. Reviews are how authors are recognized. By leaving me a review, you are paying the love forward and helping others in the process. I appreciate the time you spent with me and I'm forever grateful. See you at the top! — Sunni

Also By Sunni T. Connor

Memoir

DAMAGED little girl (Book 1)

A Damaged Woman (Book 2)

Fiction

Damien's Secret (Book 1)

Damien's Secret (Book 2)

Nonfiction

Society Vs You

Books Also Available in Spanish

About The Author

I guess I should tell you something about me. But, then again, I'm not too good at following the rules, am I? I think it's safe to say, you know enough and this journey was never about me anyway. It was always about *YOU!*

Private Coaching with Sunni

Are you tired of feeling stuck and uninspired? Want to level up your life and become the badass you were always meant to be? Look no further! As your personal mindset coach, I'll help you kick those self-doubts to the curb and unleash your full potential. We'll work together to manifest more money, more freedom, and more connection to the universe than you ever thought possible.

Plus, I promise to sprinkle in some humor and fun along the way, because who says personal growth has to be all serious and boring? So, if you're ready to ditch the limiting beliefs and start living your best life, let's do this thing! Use the QR code to go directly to the booking page, or you can also visit my website at

www.sunnitconnor.com. I can't wait to work with you!

Made in the USA
Monee, IL
04 May 2023